Discover Your Roots with the Ultimate Genealogy Tools

Gerrard .I Bloom

All rights reserved. Copyright © 2023 Gerrard .I Bloom

Funny helpful tips:

Incorporate a balanced intake of macronutrients; proteins, fats, and carbohydrates all play essential roles in health and fitness.

Stay true to your word; integrity builds trust and respect.

Discover Your Roots with the Ultimate Genealogy Tools : Uncover Your Ancestry Through Powerful Genealogy Techniques and Resources

Life advices:

Rotate between reading and listening; audiobooks offer a different experience and can be consumed on the go.

Engage with advancements in drone technology; from delivery to surveillance, drones are finding diverse applications.

Introduction

Welcome to this book, a comprehensive resource to help you uncover your family history and build your family tree using online research tools and strategies. Whether you're a beginner or an experienced genealogist, this book aims to provide you with the knowledge and techniques needed to navigate the vast world of online genealogy and discover your ancestral roots.

We'll start by introducing you to the basics of family tree research and guiding you through the initial steps of planning your genealogy project. You'll learn what a family tree is, how to collect and organize information, and how to create your first family tree. We'll also discuss the importance of recording your personal story and gathering information from family members through interviews and research.

Searching for ancestors online requires a combination of effective search techniques and the use of various tools and databases. We'll explore search engine basics, including search operators and special commands that can help you refine your results. You'll learn how to creatively search for names and connect with living relatives who can provide valuable information and insights.

The internet is a treasure trove of genealogical resources, and we'll guide you through the process of exploring online databases and websites. We'll provide an overview of free databases such as RootsWeb and the USGenWeb Project, as well as subscription sites like GenealogyBank. You'll also learn how to utilize death records, obituaries, newspapers, census records, and other valuable sources of information.

Military records often hold significant details about your ancestors, and we'll show you how to mine the web for military records, including compiled military service records, pensions, and bounty land warrants. We'll focus on the Revolutionary War and the Civil War, providing tips and resources for discovering ancestors who served during these periods.

As a nation of immigrants, tracing your immigrant ancestors is a crucial aspect of genealogical research. We'll discuss methods for finding the birthplace of your immigrant ancestor, delve into passenger lists and immigration records, and explore resources for locating records abroad, including Canada, Mexico, Central America, and South America.

Collaboration and networking play a vital role in genealogy research. We'll guide you through the process of reaching out to others in the genealogy community through message boards, mailing lists, and online archives. You'll also learn how to utilize family trees at websites like FamilySearch and Ancestry.com to connect with other researchers and expand your family tree.

To dig deeper into your family history, we'll explore additional resources such as books, magazines, blogs, occupational records, membership organizations, and photographs. We'll provide tips for evaluating the information you find and proving your research arguments. Additionally, we'll discuss strategies for overcoming obstacles when you can't find the information you're looking for.

Finally, we'll address the importance of protecting your family history from disasters and provide guidance on backing up your computer files, duplicating and distributing your research, and safeguarding your work from potential risks.

By the end of this book, you'll be equipped with the knowledge and tools to conduct effective online genealogy research, build your family tree, and uncover the stories of your ancestors. Whether you're interested in tracing your lineage for personal fulfillment or connecting with relatives and preserving your family's heritage, this guide will support you in your journey to discover your past.

Contents

CHAPTER 1: Click into Your Past 1
Family Tree Basics 1
Plan Your Project 2
What Is a Family Tree? 3
What Next? Basic Research Steps 5
Collect Information 7
Organize the Search 10
Download or Purchase a Genealogy Program 10
A Research Log Is Essential 13
Taking Good Notes Will Improve Results 14
Tame the Paper Monster 16
Record Your Progress 17
Record Names in Their Natural Order 18
Record Dates Carefully to Avoid Confusion 20
Record Places from the Smallest Jurisdiction to theLargest 21
Document Your Findings 22
CHAPTER 2: Begin Backward 26
Interview Yourself 26
Create Your First Family Tree 27
Record Your Personal Story 28
Rummage Through the Attic 30
Question Your Family Members 32
Decide Who to Interview First 33
Prepare for a Successful Interview 35

Don't Believe Every Story You Hear	37
Family Interviews Aren't a One-Time Deal	38
Has It Already Been Done?	38
Look for Published Family Histories	39
Seek Out Manuscript Collections	41
From One Generation to the Next	42
CHAPTER 3: Learn How to Search	44
Search Engine Basics	44
Other Facts Help Narrow the Search	45
Use Search Operators to Focus Results	46
Restrict Your Search with Special Commands	48
Soundex Explained	48
Get Creative with Names	52
Connect with Living Kin	54
Search Tools and Strategies	55
Bring Back Sites from the Dead	55
Use the Find Feature in Your Browser	56
Search the Web with a Toolbar	57
Use the Steve Morse One-Step Search Tools	57
Find the Right Tree in the Forest	58
CHAPTER 4: Online Starting Points	60
What Is and Is Not Online	60
Explore Free Databases	61
Root Around at RootsWeb	61
Find Local Records at the USGenWeb Project	62
Look in Lineage-Linked Databases	63
Seek Out Subscription Sites	65

GenealogyBank	67
WorldVitalRecords	68
Family Tree Connection	69
Find Family at FamilySearch	69
Just Enter a Name	70
Make Use of the Family History Library Catalog	71
Borrow Microfilm	73
Access Helpful Research Tools and Guidance	73
Discover History at the National Archives	74
Look at the Library of Congress	75
Search State Libraries and Archives	76
CHAPTER 5: Dig into Death Records	78
A Good Place to Begin	78
Search for Obituaries	79
Look Online	80
Locate Newspaper Web Sites	82
Look for a Library Web Site	83
Utilize Your Local Library	83
Social Security Death Index	83
What You Will Find in the SSDI	84
What You Won't Find in the SSDI	84
How to Search the SSDI	84
Order a Copy of the Social Security Application	85
Death Certificates and Online Indexes	86
Visit Virtual Cemeteries and Funeral Homes	88
Virtual Cemeteries Have Their Shortcomings	89
Find Online Cemetery Databases and Lists	90

Don't Disregard Funeral Home Records..91
Put It into Practice..93
CHAPTER 6: Check the Census 98
The U.S. Federal Census 98
Exploring the U.S. Federal Census 99
What the Census Can Tell You about Your Ancestors.......................................100
Access Digital Census Images Online..101
HeritageQuest Online..104
Find Free Census Alternatives 106
Check Census Gateway Sites 107
View the 1880 U.S. Federal Census at FamilySearch 107
Search or Browse the USGenWeb Census Project 108
Access Census Records Online Through Your LocalLibrary 109
Census Research Tips and Caveats 109
Learn Creativity and Patience...111
Expect Little from the 1890 Federal Census 111
Explore the Community...112
Pay Attention to Penmanship 113
Tax Lists as a Census Alternative 113
Go to the Original Record When Possible..113
Use City and County Directories...114
Put It into Practice..115
CHAPTER 7: Hunt Down Family Connections..119
Marriage and Divorce Records 119
Birth and Baptismal Records 123
Unearth Wills and Estate Records..124
Chase Down Court Records 128

Identify Adoptions and Orphans 130
CHAPTER 8: Look Local 134
Maps and Geography 134
Locate a Lost Town, Village, or Creek 135
Explore the Lay of the Land — Virtually 136
Land and Property Records 137
Who Owned the Land First? 139
Dig for Deeds 142
Locate Land Records Online 143
Historical Newspapers 146
ProQuest Historical Newspapers 148
NewspaperARCHIVE 149
Ancestry.com Historical Newspapers 149
GenealogyBank 150
Chronicling America: Historical American Newspapers 150
SmallTownPapers 151
Newspaper Abstracts 151
Libraries and Societies 151
Churches and Schools 154
Religious Records 154
School Records 157
Local History 158
CHAPTER 9: Mine the Web for Military Records 161
Find Clues to Military Service 161
Compiled Military Service Records 163
Pensions and Bounty Land Warrants 166
Discover Revolutionary and Civil War Ancestors 168

The American Revolution	169
The Civil War	171
Research Twentieth-Century Conflicts	174
Was He Drafted?	174
Request Your Ancestor's Military Service Record	177
Search Conflict-Specific Databases	178
Bone Up on Battle and Unit Histories	178
CHAPTER 10: A Nation of Immigrants	180
Find the Birthplace of Your Immigrant Ancestor	180
Plunge into Passenger Lists	182
Passenger Arrivals Prior to 1820	182
Customs Passenger Lists, 1820–1891	184
The U.S. Immigration Service Assumes Control in 1891	185
Locate Passenger Records Online	188
Emigration (Outbound) Lists	191
Border-Crossing Records — Canada and Mexico	193
Naturalization Records	194
Were They Eligible, or an Exception?	196
Not All Aliens Were Naturalized	198
Ethnic Research	200
Put It into Practice	201
CHAPTER 11: Reach Out to Others	205
Make the Most of Boards and Lists	205
Join a Genealogy Mailing List	205
Delve into Genealogy Message Boards	207
Search the Archives	209
Ferret Out Family Trees	209

Find Family Trees at FamilySearch	210
Member Trees at Ancestry.com	211
GenCircles Global Tree	211
Take Your Search Global at GeneaNet.org	212
Search the Social Networks	212
Find Family Trees by Subscription	213
Ask the Right Way	214
Share Your Research	217
Take a Class	219
Get Started for Free	220
Learn from the National Genealogical Society (NGS)	220
Enjoy an Online School Setting with GenClass	220
Earn College Credit or Enroll in a Certificate Program	221
Connect with the Pros	221
Join a Society	222
Hire a Professional	224
CHAPTER 12: Dig Deeper	226
Books, Magazines, and Blogs	226
Books	227
Magazines	228
Blogs	229
Occupational Records	229
Membership Organizations	233
Photos and Postcards	236
Locate Photographs Online	238
Who Are Those People?	240
Save Your Family Photos Before It's Too Late!	241

DNA and Genetic Genealogy 242
Paternal Ancestry — Y-DNA 244
Maternal Ancestry — Mitochondrial DNA 246
Use DNA Testing to Learn about Your Roots..248
Join a Surname Project..248
Create a Medical Family Tree..249
CHAPTER 13: Locate Records Abroad..250
A Nation of Immigrants 250
Canada...250
Mexico, Central America, and South America..253
Find Births and Marriages at FamilySearch 254
Are You Eligible for the Aztec Club of 1847? 254
Locate Country-Specific Resources at GenWeb 255
British Isles...255
Census Records...256
Civil Registration Records — Births, Marriages, and Deaths....................................259
Births, Marriages, and Deaths in Parish Records 263
The Rest of Europe 265
Ferret Out Family History in France 265
Seek Your Ancestry in Italy..267
Search for Roots in Scandinavia 268
Dig Deep for Your German Roots..270
Explore Your Eastern and Central European Heritage 272
Australia and New Zealand..274
Asia and Africa...276
CHAPTER 14: Putting It All Together 278
Evaluate What You've Found 278

What Does the Document Say?	278
Prove Your Argument	281
You Can't Find Them! Now What?	283
Protect Your Family History from Disaster	287
Back Up Your Computer Files	287
Duplicate and Distribute	288
Don't Overlook the Hidden Dangers	288
Publish Your Family History	290
Write It Down	290
Scrapbooking Your Family History	291
Share Your Family History Online	292
Dos and Don'ts of Online Genealogy	294
Do Look for Source Documentation	295
Don't Expect to Find Everything Online	295
Do Your Homework Before Forking Over Your Money	295
Don't Expect to Do It All for Free	296
Do Protect the Living When Publishing Online	296
Don't Import a GEDCOM into Your Main Family Tree File	296
Do Give Back to the Genealogy Community	297
Don't Assume That Information on the Internet Is in the Public Domain	297
Do Back Up Your Data on a Regular Basis	297
Don't Give Up	297

CHAPTER 1: Click into Your Past

Paper is the past. Digital is the future. New technologies, ranging from the Internet to digital photography, have spawned an explosion in the popularity of genealogy. Software simplifies storing, organizing, and retrieving family tree data. Images of original records long locked away in archives can be viewed online. Research guides, databases, and the expertise of other genealogists are all readily available at the click of a mouse. In short, research can be conducted more quickly, and data is much more readily available to anyone with an interest in their past.

Family Tree Basics

Millions of digitized images, from marriage certificates to military service records, can be viewed online. Published genealogies allow budding family historians to seemingly extend their family tree by generations in just a few minutes. There is even free online software available to help you record the information you find and build your family tree. It sounds so easy, right?

As valuable as the Internet is for family history research, it does have its limitations. Most importantly, don't expect to find your family tree already done for you. The Internet is just one of many research tools and resources you'll utilize in the discovery of your past. For every genealogical record that you find online, thousands more are only available in libraries, archives, courthouses, and other repositories. Much of the genealogy information published online comes in the form of indexes or transcriptions, which also requires further research in original records. And, of course, not everything located online is correct, necessitating research in additional sources to successfully prove your family connections. Yes, the Internet will simplify and enhance your quest for your roots, but it should be considered a valuable supplement to more traditional methods of research, not the sole tool for tracing your family tree.

But don't let these caveats discourage you. You *can* successfully use the Internet to plug into your past. Before you begin, however, you first need to learn a few tools of the trade — the symbols, terms, and conventions used by genealogists to collect, record, and communicate the relationships in a family tree. Some of the information presented in this introductory chapter may seem a bit complex at first, but after you spend a little time tracing your family tree it will all start to come together.

Plan Your Project

Why are you interested in your family history? Are you curious about the origin of your last name? Do you want to learn more about greatgrandpa's Polish roots? Are you hoping to identify as many of your ancestors as possible? Has an interesting story been handed down in your family that you want to pursue? Defining what you hope to learn on this journey is an important first step.

Even if your goal is to trace your entire family tree, it is practical to begin with one family line at a time. Otherwise, your research will quickly lead you into a bewildering maze of branching lineages. Go back just three generations in your own family tree, and you'll find yourself faced with researching the genealogy of eight great-grandparents. One family tree has now branched into eight, and it continues to multiply from there. By the time you've worked your way through ten generations of your family, you'll have discovered more than 1,000 ancestors!

E-LINK

As you research your family tree you may encounter numerous words with which you are unfamiliar — words specific to family history, as well as unfamiliar acronyms, and legal and Latin terms commonly encountered in genealogical records. Look them up in online genealogy glossaries such as the ones listed under Specialized Dictionaries for Genealogists (http://genealogy.about.com/od/glossaries) at About.com Genealogy.

What Is a Family Tree?

There are several different approaches you can take when beginning a family tree. A few of the more popular examples are detailed below, but pretty much anything related to researching something in the history of your family qualifies as genealogy. The format you choose to follow should be based on your individual research goals.

Direct Lineage

A direct lineage, alternately called a pedigree or ascendant tree, typically begins with you, a parent, or grandparent, and then follows a single surname or bloodline back through several generations in a direct line. This can also be expanded to include multiple direct lines, both of your parents, both of their parents, and so on. This is what most people think of when they refer to a family tree.

Family Lineage

Take the direct lineage family tree and throw in siblings; the siblings of your parents (your aunts and uncles), the siblings of your grandparents (your great-aunts and -uncles), and so on. This type of genealogy provides a more complete picture of the "family" going back through generations, rather than focusing only on the individuals from whom you directly descend.

Descendant Tree

A descendancy is the reverse of the traditional family tree. It usually starts with an ancestral couple pretty far back in the family tree and works forward to the present, attempting to account for all known descendants in all lines, both male and female. This is usually done as the next step after researching from the present back to the ancestral couple, and is a popular approach for published family histories and for those looking to find relatives to plan a family reunion.

Collateral Genealogy

Basically an extension of the direct lineage, a collateral genealogy includes additional relatives who descend from the same common ancestor through lines other than your direct line. This goes a step further than the family lineage above, including relatives such as half- and step-siblings, and the spouses and children of siblings. This type of family tree can get big and complicated, so most people primarily use collateral line research as an approach for getting around a brick wall in their direct line.

Cluster Genealogy

This is more a type of research than a family tree format, but is included here because it may affect how you plan your research project. Like collateral genealogy, cluster genealogy branches out beyond your direct lineage to include other individuals and families that were connected to your ancestors. Collateral genealogy is a type of cluster genealogy, but cluster genealogy can also mean researching neighbors, family friends, or other individuals who interacted with your ancestors. Usually it is used as a work-around approach when records on your own ancestors are lacking, but some people actually focus their research on a group of unrelated but connected people, such as members of a particular town or school.

What Next? Basic Research Steps

The typical family tree ends up incorporating elements of most of the approaches discussed in the previous section, so just consider these as a starting point for your research. The point is to begin by selecting a particular individual, couple, or family line that you want to research. Once you've selected this starting point, genealogy research follows a fairly standard set of steps.

1. **What do you want to know first?** Review the information that you have collected to date to determine what you already know about your ancestor and what you still have left to learn. From there, select a fact that you want to uncover.

2. **Identify a possible record or source for the information.** If you want to learn a death date, you might want to search for a death record or obituary. If you're looking for the names of a couple's children, you may want to begin by searching for the family in the census.

3. **Locate and search the record or source.** Determine where and how you can access the record or source. Later in this book you'll learn about hundreds of online record sources you can use for this research step. Then search for your ancestor in the record. If you have trouble locating him or her, use the search strategies discussed in Chapter 3.

4. **Copy any pertinent information.** Transcribe and/or abstract the important details from the document or source, or make a photocopy. If it is a digital image or a Web page, print a copy or save it to your computer. If the source contains no information on your ancestor, make a note to that effect.

5. **Did you find what you were looking for?** If you found the fact(s) you were looking for, move on to the next step. If not, go back to Step 2 and identify another source that may offer the information you hope to find. Since you can't always expect to find what you're looking for the first time, be prepared to cycle through Steps 2 through 5 several times.

6. **Analyze and evaluate the new information.** Look at how the fact you uncovered relates to what you already know. Does it answer your question? Does the new fact match up with everything else you know about the individual? Is the source a credible one? Use this new information to decide what you need to research next.

7. **Organize and record your results.** If you don't write down where you found a particular piece of information, or add that printout to the pile of papers on your desk, you'll eventually find yourself overwhelmed. Your brain just can't hold it all. Most genealogists use a research log or genealogy software to keep track of the sources they've searched and the information they've found.

If you've answered the question you formulated in Step 1, select a new goal and begin the genealogical research process over again. If you haven't yet met your research goal, or feel that you need further evidence to support your findings, return to Step 2 and select a new record or source. If you've tried every source you can think of and still haven't found the answer you seek, don't get discouraged. At least you've learned where the answer isn't!

Collect Information

Written records are the foundation of genealogy research, documenting the vital events in an individual's life, from birth to marriage to burial. They also provide data on property ownership, military service, taxation, school attendance, census enumeration, memberships, and other important aspects of day-to-day life. These records, whether created by governments, organizations, or private institutions, are where you'll find many of the details about your ancestors. Documentary evidence of your relatives may also be found in other, less "official" sources, including newspapers, photographs, tombstones, family bibles, school yearbooks, church membership lists, and even oral family histories.

A digital image that has been scanned or created from an original source is generally considered by genealogists as equivalent to the original as long as no evidence suggests that the image has been manipulated or altered, other than to enhance readability. Thus, there is generally no need to view both the microfilm and digitized version of the same record, unless there's a legibility issue or something appears to be missing.

The sources you'll encounter in your genealogy research can generally be classified as either *original* or *derivative*. These are a little different than the terms *primary source* and *secondary source* that you may be used to, because they refer to the physical form and provenance of a document or record, not the information that it contains.

- An **original source** is one that exists as it was originally recorded. Examples might include an oral recorded history, a handwritten will, a baptism recorded in the church records, a diary, or a photograph.

- A **derivative source** is produced by reproducing some or all of the content contained in an original source. Photocopies, abstracts, extracts, transcriptions, databases, indexes, and authored works such as genealogies and histories are generally considered to be derivative sources, as is most information found on the Internet. Examples include a transcript of an obituary, a database of marriage records, or a published genealogy.

Whenever possible, it is best to view the original source. Each time a record is transcribed, copied, or manipulated in some way there is a chance for errors to creep in. Handwriting can be difficult to interpret. Typographical errors are easy to make. Vital information can easily be skipped by accident or left out because it isn't considered important.

QUESTIONS?

How reliable is information found on the Internet?

The majority of the records you'll deal with will be derivative sources, but this doesn't necessarily mean they are unreliable. It is best, however, to consider such information as a clue for further research, and not a statement of absolute fact. Look for a citation to the original source from which the information was derived so you can evaluate the source for yourself.

Most genealogists use the terms *primary* and *secondary* to classify information, rather than sources. This is because any single source may include both primary information and secondary information.

- **Primary information** is generally provided close to the time of an event, by someone with firsthand knowledge of the reported fact(s). A birth date recorded on the birth certificate by a doctor or parent present at the birth is an example of primary information.

- **Secondary information** is provided by someone with second-hand knowledge of the reported fact(s) or is information that was recorded long after the event occurred. A birth date recorded on a death certificate by a child of the deceased is an example of secondary information. This doesn't mean the information is incorrect, just that there is more of a chance that it could be.

Each fact or piece of information found within a source needs to be evaluated separately to determine whether it is primary or secondary. This classification doesn't refer to the accuracy of the information — it refers to the *likelihood* of its accuracy. The quality or weight of the information should also be further assessed based on who provided the information, knowledge of the informant, and how closely the information correlates with information provided by other sources. Secondhand information is often correct. And firsthand information can sometimes be inaccurate. A group of people who experienced a car accident firsthand, for example, will often tell slightly different versions of the story. In another case, a couple may have moved back their marriage date by a few months when they recorded it in the family bible, to cover up an out-of-wedlock birth.

Organize the Search

As your tree starts to bear fruit, you'll find that a computer can be of tremendous help in organizing your research and presenting your results. Some traditional organization of paper files and documents will still likely be necessary, but organization of your overall research is much more important, and this is where the computer can really shine. Not only does it take up much less space than piles of papers and boxes of documents, but a computer also makes it easier to search and sort through your family tree.

Download or Purchase a Genealogy Program

Family tree software is much easier to use than pencil and paper once your family tree begins to grow. Computer software allows you to type in the name, date, and other information on each individual just once; easily move back and forth between generations in your family tree; view and print a variety of reports on your ancestors; and exchange information with family members and other researchers.

And since there are a number of good programs available for free, there really is no reason not to use genealogy software.

GEDCOM, an acronym for **Genealogical Data Communication**, is a special file format that can be read by most genealogy programs, allowing easy transfer of your family tree file from one program to the other. Learn how to open and read a GEDCOM file, as well as how to use your family tree program to create and share your own, in GEDCOM 101 (*http://genealogy.about.com/library/weekly/aa110100a.htm*).

For those of you wondering which genealogy software is the best, there really isn't a clear-cut answer. Most genealogy programs today offer good, basic functionality, so your choice should really depend upon your individual goals and preferences. Some family tree software excels at publishing books or charts. Other programs do a better job at helping you organize and document your data. The best option is to try before you buy. Most companies that sell genealogy software have a Web site where you can download a free trial or demo version. Some programs, such as Personal Ancestral File (PAF) and the standard version of Legacy Family Tree, are free. There are dozens of genealogy software programs available, but the following are some of the ones you'll most commonly encounter:

- Ancestral Quest (*www.ancquest.com*)

- Brother's Keeper (*www.bkwin.org*)

- DoroTree Jewish Genealogy Software (*www.dorotree.com*)

- Family Tree Builder (*www.myheritage.com/family-tree-builder*)

- Family Tree Maker (*www.familytreemaker.com*)

- Genbox Family History (*www.genbox.com*)

- Legacy Family Tree (*www.legacyfamilytree.com*)

- The Master Genealogist (*www.whollygenes.com*)

- Personal Ancestral File (*www.familysearch.com*)

- RootsMagic (*www.rootsmagic.com*)

There are some excellent options for Macintosh users as well, including:

- Heredis Mac X.2 (*www.myheredis.com*)

- Mac Family Tree (*www.onlymac.de/indexe.htm*)

- Reunion (Macintosh) (*www.leisterpro.com*)

E-LINK

For assistance with choosing genealogy software, ConsumerSearch *(www.consumersearch.com)* offers an excellent annual roundup of reviews of the most common genealogy programs from a variety of reviewers, including an excellent discussion of the pros and cons of each one. Type *genealogy software* into the search box to locate the genealogy section.

A Research Log Is Essential

Whether you keep it on paper or on your computer, a research log is essentially a place where you keep track of your research, from the planning stage through to completion — essentially a journal of your research process. You use it to record what you are planning to look for and where you plan to look for it. After you search the source, you add information about when you searched, what names and name variations you searched for, and what you did and did not find. You may also choose to include a record of any correspondence (e-mails, letters, etc.) in your research log, although some genealogists choose to maintain a separate correspondence log. You can track all of your research in one big research log, or maintain separate research logs for each individual, family group, or surname.

A number of software offerings allow you to view and edit your family tree online, an alternative to traditional standalone software. This is an excellent option for families or groups who are collaborating together on a genealogy. Some programs require you to host your own Web site, while others host your site on their server. Some options include Ancestry Member Trees (*http://trees.ancestry.com*), PhpGedView *(www.phpgedview.net)*, and the Next Generation (TNG) (*http://lythgoes.net/genealogy/software.php*).

Right now, as you're just setting out on your family tree journey, a research log approach may seem like a waste of time. But chances are that after you've spent a few weeks and months researching online, you'll end up visiting the same places again and again. That's not to say that you shouldn't revisit Web sites. Most are continually adding new information, and you'll also keep discovering new ancestors to research. But unless you keep track of where you've been and who and what you've searched for, you can end up wasting a lot of time and effort retracing your previous trail.

You can find a variety of research log forms online for free download, or you can easily design your own. Many genealogy software programs also offer a simple to-do list or research log feature. The goal is to keep track of the research you've done and plan to do, and whatever format is the easiest for you to use and maintain is the one you should use.

Taking Good Notes Will Improve Results

You don't want to have to rely on your memory for vital details, so consider using your computer or a notebook to take notes. Most genealogical software has a special space for notes on each individual, and some include a notes field for each individual event as well. Always label your notes with the date and place where they were taken, as well as a complete reference, or citation, to the original source.

Part of taking good notes is learning how to copy the information you find in documents and other source materials. This copying can take a number of forms, but the three most common are transcripts, abstracts, and extracts.

- A **transcript (transcription)** is a complete, word-for-word copy of the original document. Everything is copied exactly as it appears, including any errors, misspellings, abbreviations, and punctuation. If something needs clarification or you want to include your interpretation of something, comments can be added in square brackets [like this], not in parentheses. This convention tells other readers that you have added the information contained within the brackets, and that it was not found in the original.

- An **abstract** is a summary of a document's essential details, including names, dates, places, and events, in the same order that they appear in the original source. Nonessential words and punctuation are omitted. As with transcriptions, copy all names, dates, and abbreviations exactly as they appear in the original.

- **Extracts** are similar to abstracts in that they include only portions of the original document text. Instead of summarizing, however, an extract is an exact word-for-word copy of a selected portion of text, set off by quotation marks. Extracts can stand alone, but you'll more commonly find them included as part of an abstract to highlight essential portions of the text.

ALERT!

Clooz is an electronic filing cabinet designed just for genealogists who prefer computer organization to paper files. It includes more than 100 templates for recording information found in a wide variety of different genealogical records, along with blank templates, source templates, and other methods of organizing the little scraps of data you come across when researching your family tree. You can download a free trial at *www.clooz.com*.

Even if you keep both digital and paper copies of original documents such as wills and land deeds, it often helps to make a full transcription and include it in the notes section of your genealogy software, or with your research, for easy reference — a transcription is much easier to read quickly than old, faded handwriting. Transcriptions and abstracts are also useful for situations in which you can't make a copy of the original document.

ESSENTIALS

While transcribing a document, if you feel the need to insert a comment, correction, interpretation, or clarification, include it in square brackets [like this], not parentheses, to avoid confusion. Bracketed question marks [?] can be substituted for letters or words that can't be interpreted, or for interpretations that are questionable.

Tame the Paper Monster

Even if you keep almost all of your genealogy research on the computer, you'll probably still have boxes and files of certificates, photocopies, photos, and other paper records generated during the course of your search. You can scan important documents and photos into your computer, of course, but even then you probably won't want to throw away the originals. Genealogists use a number of different systems for organizing their files, including folders, binders, and notebooks. You can find an overview of several common filing systems online — just type *genealogy organization* into your favorite search engine. The books *Organizing Your Family History Search* by Sharon DeBartolo Carmack and *The Organized Family Historian* by Ann Carter Fleming, CG, CGL, offer additional organization examples and advice.

Record Your Progress

A family tree is basically one big puzzle. If you don't put the puzzle pieces together in just the right way, you'll never get to see the final picture. To help fit all of the puzzling clues together, genealogists use a variety of charts and forms to record their research data. The chart most people begin with is the pedigree chart or ancestor chart. This chart begins with you, or the individual whose ancestry you're tracing, and then branches with each generation to display the line of your direct ancestors. Pedigree charts come in a wide variety of shapes, sizes, and styles. The most common is a four-generation chart on standard 8½" × 11" paper. Some charts squeeze five or six generations into the same space, but necessarily include less room for information about each ancestor. Large wall-size ancestor charts can be printed from many genealogy software programs and then cut and pasted together, or you can order a specially printed wall chart of your family tree from a chart-printing service (great for family reunions).

E-LINK

A variety of free genealogy forms can be downloaded online for your personal use, including ancestor or pedigree charts, family group sheets, research logs, and census extraction forms. *Family Tree Magazine (www.familytreemagazine.com/forms/download.html)* and About.com Genealogy (http://genealogy.about.com/od/free_charts) offer a nice variety. Enter genealogy charts in your favorite search engine to find even more genealogy charts and forms.

The other commonly encountered genealogy form is the family group sheet. This form focuses on a family unit, with space for recording a couple and their children, including birth, death, and marriage events for each individual. Generally, these two forms work in conjunction. The pedigree chart provides the overall picture of the family tree, with links between generations, while the family group sheet records additional family details for each couple or marriage recorded on the pedigree chart.

Most genealogists follow certain standard conventions when recording data, whether on a paper chart or in their genealogy software program. By following these conventions, you help to ensure that the information you record is as complete as possible, easy to understand, and not open to misinterpretation.

Record Names in Their Natural Order

Enter the first name (also referred to as a given name or forename), followed by the middle name and surname or last name. Married women are recorded under the last name they were born with — their maiden name — not the last name they took when they got married. In situations where you wish to include both last names (such as in a written family history), you can enclose the maiden name in parentheses prior to the married name. In general, however, it is best to avoid this practice as it can confuse people as to which name is which.

While it is not necessary, most genealogists record surnames in capital letters. This makes it easy to distinguish surnames at a glance when scanning pedigree charts or genealogy queries. If you're using genealogy software, it is usually better not to enter the surname in caps, as most programs will allow you to choose how you want the names printed in charts or reports. Entering last names in lowercase allows for greater flexibility.

Naming conventions also exist for certain special situations. Again, if you're using genealogy software you won't need to worry about most of these.

- When a woman has married several times, enter her given name followed by her maiden name in parentheses, followed by the last names of her husbands in order of marriage. (Don't do this if you are using genealogy software, as you'll enter each marriage and husband separately and record the wife only under her maiden name.) Example: Linda Michelle (Koth) GARDNER MITCHELL

- Enter nicknames in quotes, not parentheses, following the given name. Genealogy software generally offers a special field in which to enter nicknames. Example: Mary "Polly" JENNINGS

- If an individual was known by more than one name because of adoption or name change, include the alternate name in parentheses following the surname. Precede the alternate name with "aka" for "also known as." If you're using a genealogy program, look for a special alternate name field. Example: William Maxwell MILLS (aka William Maxwell CRISP)

- If the surname spelling has been changed, you can record the earlier surname first, followed by the more current usage. Alternately, you can just record the surname for each individual as they commonly spelled it. Example: Stanislaw TOMAN/THOMAS

ALERT!

Almost all genealogy software programs will allow you to print out a pedigree chart, family group sheet, or other family tree chart that includes any group of people that you select. Most also offer a variety of blank forms for you to print and fill in by hand.

Record Dates Carefully to Avoid Confusion

In the United States dates are written differently than in most other parts of the world. Americans are used to dates with the month first, followed by the day and year — as in July 9, 1971. In most other countries, the same date would be written as 9 July 1971, with the day first. Both dates are easy to understand when they are written out as in the above examples, but when you see a date written

7/9/71 do you interpret it as July 9, 1971 or September 7, 1971? Or could the year be 1871 or 1771? To avoid confusion in family histories, genealogists conventionally follow the day, month, and year format for all dates, with the year written out in full. Months are generally written out in full as well, although standard three-letter abbreviations may be used.

There will be plenty of occasions in your research when you will only have an approximate date for an event. In such situations you can specify the date as "about" (abt. 1890) or "circa" (c. 1890). If you are able to narrow a date down to a specific time span (e.g., your ancestor most likely died between the day when he signed his will and the date the will was admitted into probate), record the time span using the abbreviation "bet." (between) followed by the two dates separated by a hyphen — as in 23 May 1789–3 June 1789. You can also record an event as occurring before or after a specific date — e.g., (bef. 18 Jan 1892) or (aft. 11 Sep 2001).

Record Places from the Smallest Jurisdiction to the Largest

In general this would mean the name of the place (town, village, or city), followed by the county or parish in which it was located, and then the state or province. The county or parish can be set off by commas or included in parentheses, as in Pittsburgh, Allegheny County, Pennsylvania, or Tarboro (Edgecombe), North Carolina.

The specific geographical divisions will be different in different countries and regions, but just apply the "smallest to largest" convention and you'll have it right. If your research is predominantly in one country, such as the United States, you don't need to record the name of that country, although you might want to record the country for locations outside of your predominant country of research to avoid confusion.

Document Your Findings

Gathering facts about your family and assembling them into a family tree is quite an accomplishment, but it is the backing up of these facts with sources that gives your research credibility. Keeping track of where you found each piece of information or statement of fact is important as a means for others to evaluate or verify your work. It also allows you to easily go back again and again, to remember where your information came from, or to confirm its reliability in your own mind. To do this, genealogists use what is called a source citation. The source is the document, database, photograph, interview, or other record in which the specific fact or information was found. The citation is the formal reference to that source, including all details necessary for someone to identify and locate the source material.

Source citations in genealogy generally follow standard bibliographic citation standards, similar to those found in *The Chicago Manual of Style*. A good rule of thumb is to work from general to specific.

- Author or compiler (the person who created the content)
- Title of the source (book, Web site, etc.)
- Publication details (place, publisher, and date)
- Specific details needed to locate the information within the source, such as page number, chapter, entry, etc.

Internet sources generally follow the same format as traditional published materials. A Web site title, for example, is equivalent to a book title. A database contained within a specific Web site can be treated as a book chapter. The publisher is the entity that owns or created the Web site, although this can be omitted if it duplicates the name of the Web site, as it does with Ancestry.com. In place of traditional publication place and date, you cite the URL of the Web site and the date on which you accessed or viewed the site. The additional details necessary for a footnote citation would include the information necessary to find the actual record, such as the individual's name and location, and the entry number.

A footnote source citation for a World War I Draft Registration Card found online at Ancestry.com might appear as follows:

> *U.S. Selective Service System, "World War I Draft Registration Cards, 1917–1918," Ancestry.com, digital images (www.ancestry.com: accessed 13 December 2007), for Claude Mancil Crisp, Edgecombe County, North Carolina; citing* World War I Selective Service System Draft Registration Cards, 191—1918, *National Archives microfilm M1509.*

Sources will use slightly different punctuation and arrangement depending on how they are used — footnote, bibliography, or in-text. The above example is a bit complicated since it references digital images, but it also fairly represents many of the genealogical databases accessed online.

Cite what you see! Many of the sources you'll be using online, such as indexes, pedigree charts, and cemetery transcriptions, have been created or "derived" from a previously existing source. While such a derivative source may include a citation to the original source of the information, you must cite what you actually "see" or use — the derivative source, not the original from which it was created. This is because derivative sources are prone to human error, including typing mistakes and misinterpreted handwriting. If such a mistake exists and you cite the original source without reference to the online derivative source where you actually found your information, others will assume that the error is yours.

Consider a situation where you locate your great-grandmother's birth date from a transcription made and posted online by the local genealogical society. In this case, you would not cite her tombstone and/or the cemetery as your source because you have not personally seen her grave marker. Instead, you would cite the online transcription created by the genealogical society.

Many people don't take the time to cite sources when they first begin researching their family tree. It's just so easy to assume that all of your data is accurate, so why does it matter where it came from? It's also easy to get caught up in the excitement of the search and tell yourself that you'll go back and do it later. Problems arise, however, when you find new information that contradicts your previously "accurate" data. Without sources, you have no way to know where you found the earlier information, which makes it difficult to resolve the discrepancy. Documenting sources for all information as it is uncovered can save many, many hours of backtracking. Source citations really are worth the extra time and effort!

Learn more about how to structure source citations in the highly regarded book by Elizabeth Shown Mills, *Evidence! Citation and Analysis* for the *Family Historian*. A second, much weightier, edition of this manual titled *Evidence Explained: Citing History Sources from Artifacts to Cyberspace* includes many additional examples for those who really appreciate step-by-step guidance.

CHAPTER 2: Begin Backward

Many people begin their family tree search knowing next to nothing about their own grandparents and great-grandparents. Sure, you know their names, and perhaps their date of birth, but do you know when they were married? What they did for a living? Where they lived when they were growing up? The names of their siblings? Without at least some basic knowledge of your family tree, you're likely to quickly find yourself spinning your wheels online. That's why a good genealogy search should always begin at home.

Interview Yourself

Why not? You probably know more about your own history than you think you do. You're probably impatient to jump right on to the Internet to find everything you can on your family, but your search will almost always bring more success if you begin at home — with yourself and your living relatives. Surfing the Internet for information on an average name will bring up some-where in the neighborhood of a million sites that may shelter tidbits about your family, and who has time to wade through all of that? The more facts you have about your family before you hit the Web, the more easily you'll be able to distinguish your ancestors from others with the same name, and the less frustrating the search will be.

ESSENTIALS

A journal or notebook can be a handy tool for recording your progress during this fact-gathering stage, including the people you talk to, the questions you ask, the information you collect, and the stories you're told. If you have family members who prefer to write rather than talk, a special memory book full of thought-provoking family history questions may provide just the inspiration they need.

Begin your family tree by writing down as much basic information as you can remember about your relatives. This might include dates and locations of birth, marriage, and death, names of spouses and children, wars in which relatives served, where they went to school, their occupation, their church and/ or religion, and any other facts that you can recall. Start with yourself or your children and then work backward through the generations to your parents and grandparents — as far back as you can go. If you can, extend the information to aunts, uncles, siblings, and other family members. Try to remember full names, including middle names, nicknames, and the maiden names for married women. If you know the exact date of an event, write it down. If you only know that it was about 1952 or sometime during World War II, write that down. Everything doesn't have to be perfect. The goal here is just to get something down on paper so that you have somewhere to start.

Create Your First Family Tree

Once you've pulled together every scrap of knowledge from your head and your home, it's time to enter the information into your computer software or a pedigree chart. This helps you see at a glance where you have gaps in your family history knowledge, which in turn can lead to questions to ask your relatives or details to look up online. Be sure to include a source for each piece of information, whether you learned it from a birth certificate or your great uncle. This may seem like a waste of time right now, but you'll appreciate it down the road when you find conflicting information — which you will. Memories are faulty, stories get embellished, and you'll probably find at least one female relative who fudged on her age.

QUESTIONS?

What if I don't like to write?

Scrapbooking offers an alternative means of sharing your personal or family history. This allows you to use photos to tell much of the story, with short notes, commonly referred to as journaling, to add additional detail. The Scrapbooking site at About.com offers a wealth of resources for creating your first scrapbook *(http://scrapbooking.about.com)*, including supply suggestions, tutorials, and layout and design ideas.

Record Your Personal Story

While you're busy reflecting on the past, it's worth taking some time to record your own story, or at least some of the major events, feelings, and experiences from your own life. It doesn't necessarily need to be done before you dig into your family history, but it's also likely to mean more to your descendants than any family tree you create ever could. It's hard to express how wonderful it is to find a journal or diary written by a long-dead ancestor. Even a simple letter in their handwriting is a treasure. To be able to read about their life in their own words, to learn how the major events experienced only through history books impacted them, to see how the names and dates discovered during research really fit into their life — that is true family history.

A personal history doesn't need to be an entire autobiography. Begin small, with some basics about yourself. Then add more stories over time. Eventually, the plan would be to cover every stage of your life: birth and childhood, family life, school years, courtship and marriage, raising your own family. Touch on all the major points — your job(s), your beliefs, your travels, your hobbies, your favorite foods — asking yourself who, what, when, where, why, and how questions about each. And don't use the excuse that your life is boring! No matter how mundane it may seem to you, a hundred years from now your stories will fascinate your descendants.

The Internet is a great source for writing prompts and inspiration for writing a personal family history, as well as journal-keeping software and services. Writing the Journey (*www.writingthejourney.com*) is a good place to begin if you are new to journal writing. The free online workshop offers questions, prompts, and exercises to assist you in telling your life story. Several subscription services, such as LifeBio (*www.lifebio.com*), offer online questions and templates to help you write your own story. They also help you publish the final version as a hardbound book if you desire. At WebBiographies (*www.webbiographies.com*) you can start a free journaling Web site, with tools and space for writing your memoirs. Links to these and similar resources can be found in the Writing Your Life Story section of About.com Genealogy (*http://genealogy.about.com/od/autobiography*).

Rummage Through the Attic

Genealogy is all about clues, and many of the best clues can be found without leaving home. Generations of family "stuff" await your discovery in attics, basements, drawers, and closets. Take a good look through your house. Most people have at least a few official documents in their home, such as birth certificates, passports, report cards, military discharge papers, or marriage certificates. Look for these and other records that might provide names, dates, and locations. But don't stop there! Pull out your family photo albums and scrapbooks. Look for old letters, newspaper clippings, and family memorabilia. Anything from your past is fair game. Label everything you recognize and add any new information to your research log or journal and your family tree.

E-LINK

Family memorabilia that has escaped the family home can sometimes be found online. The National Genealogical Society *(www.ngsgenealogy.org)* maintains an online database of over 3,100 bibles for its members. Family records, photos, and heirlooms can often be found on auction sites such as eBay *(www.ebay.com)*, or on Lost and Found sites *(http://genealogy.about.com/od/orphan_photos)* where people post family items they have rescued from flea markets and antique stores.

Even if you can find no real genealogical treasures in your own home, you might be surprised what lurks in the homes of your relatives. They may be surprised too! Family history can be found in unusual places — the hem of a quilt, the back of a photo, a locket inscription. Photos and albums help match names with faces. If pictures aren't labeled, ask your relatives to help you with identification. Family bibles often contain information about marriages, births, baptisms, deaths, and other important family events. Letters and postcards may be filled with family news and stories, and the date and postmark may provide clues as to where your family lived at a given time. If your family has been in the same home for generations, even the walls can talk. You may find notes recorded on the inside of closet doors, growth charts penciled on the walls, or old newspapers used for insulation in the attic. Ask your relatives if they will agree to go through their house with you, as this allows you to easily ask questions about anything you find. If this isn't possible, however, here are some things you might ask your relatives to look for.

- Important papers (birth certificates, wills, naturalization documents, titles, and deeds)

- Pictures, photo albums, scrapbooks, baby books

- Newspaper clippings

- Bibles

- Letters and postcards

- Diaries and journals

- Books (check for inscriptions)

- Funeral and Mass cards

- Family trees

- School papers, including report cards and yearbooks

- Awards and certificates

- Quilts, samplers, or other needlework

- Jewelry (check for inscriptions)

Your relatives may be understandably reluctant to let precious family records or mementos out of their possession, so consider bringing a portable scanner and a laptop with you on your attic hunt. A good digital camera can also do the trick. This way you'll have digital copies of everything for your records, and to easily share with the rest of the family. Take good notes, and transcribe any documents in case your pictures or scans don't turn out as well as expected.

Question Your Family Members

There's nothing quite as deflating as calling your grandmother to share your latest genealogy "find" only to have her reply, "I could have told you that." Your family members represent a vast source of untapped knowledge about your family history, and questioning them will likely turn up countless interesting details. Contact everyone you can think of, from your ninety-eight-year-old great-grandma to the second cousin you haven't seen since you were kids. Even friends of the family can provide useful details. Everyone, both the old and the young, will have different memories and perspectives. They may recall the same event in a different way, have interacted with different family members, or be able to provide details that no one else can. You probably won't get to them all before the urge to jump on the Internet finally gets the better of you, but try to talk to as many as you can.

Talking to your family members can mean anything from a formal recorded interview to a casual conversation over the dinner table, or even an occasional question asked by e-mail. The casual conversation approach works especially well, as it seems to put family members more at ease. The downside, however, is that you don't always get the chance to take notes right away, and have no recording to fall back on. A nice compromise is to set up a video camera on a tripod in the corner of the dining room or other room where the interviewee feels comfortable, and then start a casual conversation about family events and memories. Your subject will often forget the camera is running (or at least stop worrying about it). If you can get two or more family members together at once, the informal conversation and memory-sharing pretty much takes care of itself. Either way, ask a few questions to get the conversation started, but don't be afraid after that point to let your relative(s) wander from one memory to the next.

ALERT!

Ancestry.com offers a nifty audio storytelling feature as part of its free online family tree service, which allows you to send an e-mail invitation, including a toll-free phone number and personalized PIN, to a family member asking them to record a memory for your online family tree. The recording(s) are saved online for you and invited family members to share and enjoy.

Decide Who to Interview First

Begin by talking to the oldest living family members, when possible, because they are the ones whose memories are most at risk of being lost forever and they usually know the most about the family. You'll often find them the easiest to talk to as well, because they have more free time and usually appreciate the fact that someone is interested in their stories. It also helps to think about what you're hoping to learn and who is most likely to have that information. If your goal is to learn your great-grandmother's maiden name, you might want to start with your grandmother, if she is still living, or one of her siblings. Or you may just want to start with the people who are most willing or interested in the information you are gathering. It's a lot easier to get information from someone who is excited about what you are doing.

Most families also have at least one person known to be the keeper of the family history — the one who has spent some time researching the family tree, who has the largest collection of family photos and memorabilia, or is just the "busybody" sort who knows everything about everyone. This is someone you're definitely going to want to talk to. He or she may not always be someone in your direct line, however, so it may take some detective work on your part. If your great-grandfather, for example, had several siblings, then descendants of any of those other children are just as likely as your grandfather to have family photos, letters, and other items that have been saved.

QUESTIONS?

What questions should I ask my relatives?

Begin by using the family tree chart you've started to create a basic list of questions. Next, add additional questions based on major life events, such as going to school and getting married — focusing not just on facts, but also on how, why, where, and with what results. Open-ended questions that require more than just a "yes" or "no" answer help encourage personal commentary.

Prepare for a Successful Interview

There are many tutorials and guides online to help you prepare for and conduct a successful oral history interview, covering such matters as what to bring with you and which questions to ask for best results. More important than all these little details, however, is actually sitting down and talking to your relatives. To get you started, here are some basics to keep in mind.

- **Check your equipment in advance.** Be sure you have paper and pencil and extra batteries, and that the equipment all works. If you can get into the room where you're going to conduct the interview, do a practice run to be sure the microphone will pick up both you and the interviewee.

- **Come prepared.** Bring a list of topics you want to cover, family group sheets or pedigree charts to be verified or expanded, and some family photos and other props to help jog your relative's memory.

- **Don't interrupt.** The best way to keep your interviewee involved is to listen to what she has to say. You can ask follow-up questions to get more details, but don't worry too much about your interview getting off track as long as your relative is still talking about the family. Sometimes those little "tangents" reveal the most interesting clues.

- **Be respectful, not pushy.** If your relative appears reluctant to give details about a particular event or person, don't press. There may be a "secret" or a painful memory, and pushing too hard can mean an end to her willingness to talk to you. Save it for a future conversation, or as something to ask other relatives about.

- **Make note of any names, places, and events mentioned during the interview.** After the interview, ask your relative to go through this list with you, to add full names with correct spellings.

- **Follow through.** If you taped the interview, make a transcript. If you took written notes, make a photocopy. Send a copy to your interviewee along with a thank-you letter.

While you're busy digging for facts to fill in the blanks of your genealogy software or family tree chart, don't forget to ask for and record the stories as well. Every family has them. Some are well-rehearsed — like the stories Grandpa likes to tell just about every time the family gets together. Others may have never been told because no one ever thought to ask. Both are an important part of the family history and deserve to be written down.

Even if you've been asking your family members questions for years, they will still manage to surprise you with new information. Don't expect to learn everything the first time you ask, and don't listen when a family member tells you they don't know anything. It may take time, patience, and creativity, but you can generally learn something useful from every living relative in your family tree.

Don't Believe Every Story You Hear

Almost all family stories have a kernel of truth, but sometimes that's about all that's true. You may hear stories of being related to a famous individual, such as Abraham Lincoln or Napoleon Bonaparte. You may be told that your great-great-grandmother was a Cherokee princess. Or you may encounter the common tradition that your family tree goes back to "three brothers" who came to America. It's possible, of course, that these stories are true. It's much more likely, however, that such stories are more myth than fact.

There's a game you may have played as a child known as "Chinese whispers" or "Telephone." A sentence or phrase is whispered into the ear of the first participant, who then whispers what he hears to the next person in line. By the time the sentence reaches the end of the line, it is often unrecognizable from the one uttered at the beginning. In the same way, family stories are often changed or embellished as they are passed down through successive generations. For this reason, all family stories and traditions should be verified through careful genealogy research before you accept them as fact. Don't laugh at the stories, however, no matter how ridiculous they may sound. Respect the feelings of those who believe them and wait to correct any misconceptions until you have evidence that disproves the family tradition.

Family Interviews Aren't a One-Time Deal

Look at every family gathering as a potential source for information.

If you're getting together for a family reunion or the holidays, e-mail your family members in advance and ask them to bring their favorite family photographs or heirlooms to share. You can even scan the collection and create a CD for everyone to take home. If your relatives have e-mail, it offers a great medium for asking a quick question about something that comes up in your research. Alternatively, you may want to try an e-mail question of the week or month — sort of an ongoing family history conversation. You can also create a private family Web site that allows your relatives to post recipes, share stories and photos, and keep up-to-date on your research. Some family sites even offer private family chat rooms, blogs, and message boards, which can be a great way to collect and preserve your family's stories. See Best Places to Put Your Family Tree Online (*http://genealogy.about.com/od/publishing/tp/web_sites.htm*) for suggestions.

Has It Already Been Done?

Even if you can't locate someone in your immediate family who has researched the family history, it doesn't mean it hasn't already been done. Most family trees have many, many branches that have spread far and wide through successive generations. This means that records that detail your family may not always be found in the possession of your relatives, or even in the area where your ancestors lived. A written family history, a collection of old family letters, or a scrapbook of ancestral photographs may have been donated to a library or repository on the other side of the country, but how do you find it?

ALERT!

Remember the old adage that just because it's in print doesn't make it true? Family histories, both published and unpublished, vary in scope and quality. Errors can be found in most such works, particularly when the author has not cited the sources of his information. For this reason, always consider compiled genealogies as secondary sources that need double-checking with primary documents.

Look for Published Family Histories

In reality, only a small percentage of families have published genealogies. It is, however, always worth a look to see if someone has compiled and published a genealogy on your family, or the family in which you're interested.

One of the best places to search for published genealogies online is the Library of Congress, which has one of the world's premier collections of genealogical and local historical publications from the United States and around the world. To find published family histories that may relate to your family, search the LOC online catalog (*http://catalog.loc.gov*) for your surname plus the term *family*, such as *powell family*. You can also search by location, such as in *westmoreland co* or *church records virginia*.

The Family History Library (see Chapter 4) also maintains a large collection of published family histories. Use the Surname search in the Family History Library Catalog to locate catalog entries for family histories and other compiled works that include a specific surname. More than 5,000 of the family history books, biographies, and diaries from this collection have been scanned and placed online in digital format by the Harold B. Lee Library at Brigham Young University as the Family History Archive (*www.lib.byu.edu/fhc*).

The Family and Local Histories Collection created by ProQuest contains over 7.5 million fully searchable pages from more than 7,200 family histories, as well as local histories and other published primary sources. This database can be accessed online through HeritageOnline, by members of subscribing libraries, as well as on Genealogy.com for individual subscribers. Ancestry.com also offers a database of family and local histories. See Chapter 4 for more information on these Web sites.

ESSENTIALS

More than 30 percent of published material related to genealogy and history, including family genealogies, can be found in genealogical and historical magazines and journals. The Periodical Source Index (PERSI), which indexes more than 5,000 such periodicals by surname and locality, can be viewed in most major libraries, and online as a searchable subscription database at Ancestry.com.

Thousands of genealogy and local history books are also available online on Google Books (*http://books.google.com*). In some cases, the entire book can be downloaded free of charge. For books still under copyright, you can generally view the index, table of contents, and selected portions of the text.

If you locate a reference to a published family history online, you'll often be able to find a copy in the collection of the local public library or genealogical society library that serves the area where your ancestors lived. Check their online catalog, if available, or e-mail them to ask if they have a copy. If they do, you can generally request copies of selected pages for a fee.

Seek Out Manuscript Collections

Manuscript materials such as unpublished family histories and collections of family and personal papers are actively collected by over 1,400 American institutions. A manuscript is basically a handwritten or typed document, as distinguished from a printed, published record. These may include personal letters and diaries, coroner's inquests, prison records, church records, and voter registration records. The difficulty lies in locating a manuscript that may be useful to you. One very handy tool for this is the National Union Catalog of Manuscript Collections (NUCMC), an index to mostly unpublished materials in both well-known and obscure repositories across the United States. NUCMC records created since 1986 can be searched on the Web site of the Library of Congress (*www.loc.gov/coll/nucmc*) through the RLG Union Catalog. NUCMC records created from 1959 to 1985 are available in printed volumes, which can be found at major libraries throughout the country. ArchivesUSA, available by annual subscription to institutions, makes all of NUCMC (1959 to the present) fully searchable online. A similar service, ArchiveGrid, includes most records from the NUCMC catalog as well. You'll usually find access to one or both of these databases available through state libraries, academic libraries, and archives.

ALERT!

Don't let the dates fool you! Dates in the National Union Catalog of Manuscript Collections (NUCMC) refer to the date the records were catalogued, not when they were created. Many older records have been added to the collection since 1986, and are available in the free version available on the Library of Congress Web site.

From One Generation to the Next

It is very tempting when you're researching your family tree to jump ahead of yourself and skip a generation or two. Imagine that you discover a census record for your grandmother living with her husband and children. But wait! You look further down and find her father living in the same house-hold. Just think, you've learned your grandmother's maiden name and her father's name in one fell swoop. You're probably already typing his name into a search box to see what else you can learn! And then there's the tale your grandfather told of his father arriving at Ellis Island as a young man of eighteen with nothing more than the clothes on his back. One of the first things you're going to want to do online is search for him in the Ellis Island database, right?

Naming patterns can sometimes help identify links between generations of a family. You may find names of grandparents, parents, aunts, and uncles repeated in succeeding generations. Occasionally you'll even find an unusual name that has survived in the family for decades. Sometimes an unusual middle name may indicate the maiden name of the mother or grandmother.

Jumping ahead of oneself is human nature. But in genealogy it can also mean disaster. By skipping a generation or two, you run the risk of identifying the wrong people as your ancestors and being tangled forever in someone else's family tree. It happens more frequently than you may think. This doesn't mean you can't pursue a new lead when it smacks you in the face, but after you've done some searching to satisfy your curiosity, go back and finish your research on the previous generation(s) to ensure that everything does indeed match up as you believe. Don't just rely on your grandmother's name and the name of her father. Identify as much as you can about your grandmother, checking all of the available records for anything you can glean. Just learning something as simple as where and when she was born can help distinguish her from others of the same name. Additional research may also provide you with the names of siblings, the birthplace of her parents, her mother's name, and other clues. This way, when you locate records for her parents, you can feel confident that you have correctly identified the next branch in your family tree.

CHAPTER 3: Learn How to Search

One of the first things many would-be family historians do when they decide to peek into their family's past is type the name of their ancestor into a major search engine or genealogy database. After sifting through thousands of irrelevant results, they throw up their hands in frustration, convinced that nothing exists online about their family. The problem with this scenario, however, isn't the lack of information; it's the technique. Strong search skills are an essential tool for successful online genealogy research.

Search Engine Basics

You wouldn't wander aimlessly through the stacks at a large city library looking for a book on your family. In the same way, you shouldn't approach a family history hunt on the Internet without a plan. Whether you're using a search engine like Google or searching for your ancestors in the Ellis Island database, an important part of online genealogy research is learning how to search. The sheer magnitude of information available online makes locating information on a particular individual a bit more complicated than just typing a name into a search engine. There are three simple ways to improve your search results: (1) choose your search terms carefully, (2) learn how to use special search operators, and (3) restrict your search with special commands.

QUESTIONS?

Which search engine is best for genealogy?

Most genealogists prefer Google *(www.google.com)*, primarily because it indexes the most pages and tends to return somewhat relevant results. Clusty *(www.clusty.com)* is also good, because as a metasearch engine it combines results from a variety of sources. You can learn more about the various search engines and their uses in Wendy Boswell's excellent guide to the Best Search Engines on the Web *(http://websearch.about.com/od/enginesanddirectories/p/websearch101.htm)*.

Other Facts Help Narrow the Search

It's always a good idea to think about your search before you begin. What do you know about your great-grandfather Jack Smith that can help you distinguish him from all the other Jack Smiths of the world? Perhaps you know that he was born in Monongahela, Pennsylvania. You also know that he married your grandmother, Cornelia, and that he was a blacksmith. Use these facts as keywords to help narrow down your search. A search for *jack smith blacksmith monongahela* or *jack smith cornelia monongahela* is much more likely to yield something about your great-grandfather than a search for just *jack smith*.

For more general results, you might try adding the word *genealogy* or *family* to your surname, as in *powell genealogy* or *owens family*.

This type of search will often bring up family history information that other researchers have posted online. To be honest, this type of search technique lends itself better to names more unique than Powell or Owens. In the above example, better results were achieved when at least one more identifying keyword was added to the search, such as *archibald powell genealogy* or *owens family edgecombe nc*.

Along these same lines, consider what you want to find. If you're looking for death information, you'll want to try the word *death* or *died* in your search. You could also try adding the word *cemetery* or *obituary* to your search query to bring up death information about your ancestor. Think about the types of words that might appear in the information you're looking for, and use these as keywords to help focus your search.

Use Search Operators to Focus Results

Most major search engines, including Google, MSN, and Yahoo!, allow you to use special search operators to focus results. These operators allow you to search for specific phrases, exclude certain words, or otherwise fashion a search query that will help you find exactly what you want.

- **Use quotation marks to find complete phrases.**
  Regular searches look for all keywords to appear on the same page, but don't pay any attention to their proximity to one another. A search for *jebediah smith* would turn up a page that contained Jebediah Brazelton and Bob Smith, neither of which are your Jebediah Smith. By enclosing specific search phrases in quotes, you force the search engine to find documents that contain the exact phrase, as in *"jebediah smith"* or *"washburn cemetery."*

- **Include the Boolean operators AND or OR between words.** As it sounds, the Boolean operator AND used between two words tells the search engine that both terms must be present on the Web page to be included in the search results. Most search engines assume an AND between keywords, or you can use the plus sign, so it isn't often necessary to use this command. The Boolean operator OR requires one term or the other to be present on a Web page, but not both. This feature can be helpful when searching for name variations *powell AND archie OR archibald* or when searching for variations of the same term *crisp AND tombstone OR gravestone*. Boolean operators must be in ALL CAPS.

- **Add a plus (+) to force certain words to be included in your search.** The plus sign is rarely needed, but can serve as a substitute for AND to ensure that all of your keywords are included in the results. So, instead of using *crisp AND cemetery AND macclesfield* you could use *crisp +cemetery +macclesfield*. There are also some small words, called stop words, that search engines commonly ignore when processing a search query. If you really need these to be a part of your search, add a plus (+) in front of them, as in *thomas jefferson +will*.

- **Add a minus (—) to exclude specific words from your search.** When your ancestor shares a name with a famous individual or a popular product, you can use this option to help direct the focus away from these irrelevant results. A search for *jimmy dean — sausage* will help eliminate results from the Jimmy Dean Foods company, while *washington — dc — george — president* will help eliminate at least some of the clutter caused by the millions of results for President George Washington.

Restrict Your Search with Special Commands

As you get more comfortable with simple searches, you might want to try your hand at more advanced techniques. Most major search engines include special commands that allow you to restrict your search in some way — to a specific site or date range, for example. The list of available search commands varies by search engine, but the most useful for genealogy purposes is the **site:** command, which restricts your search results to a specific Web site or domain. The search command *"james brown" site:* www.archives.gov, for example, would restrict the search results for the phrase *james brown* to return only pages from the Web site of the National Archives. You can also use this command to restrict your searches to sites with a specific domain extension — a search for *vital records site:.gov* will return matches for vital records only on sites in the .gov, or government, domain. Check your favorite search engine's help page to learn what commands are available and become familiar with them.

To eliminate the need to remember all of these search options, you can also use the search engine's advanced search page. Most allow you to use all of the features discussed above by selecting variables from a drop-down list or clicking a check box. Check the search engine's home page for a link to Advanced Search.

Soundex Explained

Soundex is a word you'll run across often when searching genealogy records. First patented by Robert C. Russell of Pittsburgh, Pennsylvania, in 1918, Soundex is a special type of coded indexing system created for use with the U.S. census and other records commonly used by genealogists. Soundex is different than a standard alphabetical index because it groups last names based on the way they sound, so that similar names will be found together regardless of how they are spelled. This helps researchers find and identify last names that appear under various spellings, such as Smith, Smyth, or Smythe.

ALERT!

While a working knowledge of Soundex coding is important for family historians, the nuances of the system can make hand-coding tricky. This is where a software conversion program, such as the RootsWeb Soundex Converter *(http://resources.rootsweb.com/cgi-bin/soundexconverter)*, comes in handy. Just enter a surname to return the Soundex code, along with a list of other names that use the same code — good for alternative spelling suggestions.

A Soundex code consists of a letter and three numbers, such as F652. The letter is always the first letter of the surname. The three numbers come from the remaining letters in the name, assigned so that letters that sound alike, and could therefore be easily confused, are given the same numerical value. Vowels (a, e, i, o, and u) and vowel-sounding consonants (h, w, and y) are eliminated from the coding process. To determine the Soundex code for a particular surname:

- Write the first letter of the surname. This is the beginning of your Soundex code.

- Assign a number to the next three letters of the surname, according to the following guide. Skip the letters not included in the chart below: A, E, I, O, U, H, W and Y.

    1 B, F, P, V

    2 C, G, J, K, Q, S, X, Z

    3 D, T

    4 L

    5 M, N

    6 R

- Disregard any remaining letters in the surname. The final Soundex code should consist of a letter and three numbers. If there are not enough consonants in the name to form the four character Soundex code, add zeros to complete it.

Additional rules and refinements include the following:

- If a name contains double letters, such as TT, treat them as a single letter and assign only one number. *Example:* The RR in Garrett would be coded as 6, not 66.

- If two or more letters represented by the same Soundex code appear in sequence, assign the number only once. *Example:* Only the C of the CKS in Dickson is coded since these adjacent letters all share the code number 2. Thus, Dickson is coded as D250, not D222.

- If a vowel (A, E, I, O, U) separates two consonants that have the same Soundex code, it is considered a separator and negates the "two or more letters" rule above. The consonant to the right of the vowel is, thus, coded. *Example:* The Soundex code for Toman is T550 (T, 5 for the M, 5 for the N, and 0 to complete the 4 character code). Since the vowel A separates the M and N, the N is coded.

- In the case of two consonants with the same code number separated by either an H or W, only the first is coded, while the second is ignored. *Example:* Ashcroft would be coded as A261. The C is ignored since H separates the S and C.

- Surnames with prefixes, such as Con, De, Le, Van, and Von, should be coded both with and without the prefix. You may find such names indexed either way in the Soundex. Note, however, that Mc and Mac are generally not considered prefixes, so their Soundex code begins with M.

Important Note: There is some discrepancy in the way the *H or W rule* has historically been interpreted in Soundex coding. For most Soundex indexes, the rule is interpreted as it was originally conceived — as discussed above. For the U.S. census, however — especially the 1880, 1900, and 1910 enumerations — the H or W was more often treated like a vowel, as a separator between two consonants sharing the same code, and both consonants were coded. Thus, the surname Ashcroft was encoded as A226, not A261 as under the original Soundex rules. When you're researching a surname that contains an H or W, your best bet is to always look for it under both Soundex codes. If you're searching in an online index with a Soundex search option, try searching for the surname both with and without the H or W.

The Daitch-Mokotoff Soundex System, developed by genealogist Gary Mokotoff and later improved by Randy Daitch, refines the way in which Slavic and Yiddish surnames are coded, making it easier to match similar-sounding names. You'll find this Soundex system in use for many online Jewish and Eastern European databases. The Avotaynu Web site *(www.avotaynu.com/soundex.htm)* includes a detailed description of the coding rules.

Using Soundex to code your surnames is not something you'll really need to do all that often. In general, most Internet databases already include some type of automatic Soundex search that uses the Soundex algorithm to bring up alternative surnames. It's useful to know, however, in case your research leads you to microfilmed records, or for situations where a traditional Soundex search just isn't turning up the records you expect to find.

Get Creative with Names

Soundex search does a good job of picking up some alternate name spellings and variations, but names can still surprise you. Your family's surname was not likely always spelled the same way that it is now. It may have been "Americanized" by your ancestors in order to help them assimilate into their new country and culture. An unusual spelling or non-Latin characters may have begged for simplification. A name change may have also arisen from a desire to conceal nationality or religious orientation for fear of reprisal or discrimination. Or your branch of the family may have just decided to change the spelling to make it easier to spell or because they liked the new name better. The point is that you need to approach names with an open mind. Some are simple spelling changes — the German surname Heyer has become Hyer, Hier, Hire, Hires, and Hiers. Other changes are more obscure, such as the surname Toman being "Americanized" to Thomas.

Misspelled names are also extremely common. Most of the records in which you'll find your ancestors were recorded by someone else — a court clerk, a priest, an immigration official — who may not have known how it was spelled. Your ancestor probably even spelled his own name in different ways at different times. Names are also often just written down wrong, by people who spelled them phonetically, or by individuals trying to transcribe messy handwriting or blurred records for an index.

When searching for your family in online databases, get creative with surname spellings. If your name is plural, such as Owens, search for both Owen and Owens. Use a wildcard in databases that allow it (many genealogy databases do, although Internet search engines generally do not), to help search for several options at once. Examples of this include *owen** to search for Owen or Owens and *john** to return surnames such as John, Johnson, Johnsen, Johnathon and Johns. For each database you search, read the instructions or look for an advanced search page to see what search options are available to you.

First names or given names are also candidates for variation. Your grandmother Elizabeth may also appear in records as Liz, Lizzie, Lisa, Beth, Eliza, Betty, or Bessie. You might also find her listed by her initial, as in E. Martin or E. R. Martin. Some people also go by their middle name; in this case she may be listed as Roberta Martin. These people can sometimes be the most tricky to find, because they'll often choose to use their given name in official records, and use the middle name that they are called in more informal situations. There are families in which all of the children are enumerated in one census by their first names, in the next census by the middle names they more commonly used, and in yet a third census by their initials. The key is to keep an open mind when searching for your ancestors, and to search for all possibilities before you give up.

Connect with Living Kin

Genealogy isn't just about locating people who have been dead for decades or centuries. It is also about connecting with living family members — to capture their stories and memories, collaborate on research, learn about new branches of the family tree, or plan a family reunion. Not surprisingly, you can apply many of the same search strategies to locate living people. There are, however, a few online tools and databases that can assist with your search.

QUESTIONS?

How can I locate information on someone who is recently deceased?

The best place to begin is the Social Security Death Index (SSDI), a database of over 80 million Americans whose deaths have been reported to the Social Security Administration. From this free index you can learn the date of death and location where the final benefit was sent, which you might then use to locate an obituary notice. Learn more in Chapter 5.

One of the most obvious places to begin a search for living individuals is the telephone directory. This may not be very fruitful if they have a common name, or if you aren't even sure which state they are in, however. If you can't locate a husband, try searching under his wife's name, and vice versa. A search by just the last name and location may also help turn up listings under initials or other first-name variations. Popular online phone directories include White Pages (*www.whitepages.com*), Yahoo! People Search (*http://people.yahoo.com*), and ZabaSearch (*www.zabasearch.com*).

Since the Internet is all about connecting the world, it's not a surprise to find so many Web sites dedicated to helping people reunite with one another. If you're searching for a military buddy, Wendy Boswell's list of Military People Search Sites (*http://websearch.about.com/od/peoplesearch/a/militarysearch.htm*) may be of some assistance. Want to connect with an old classmate? Then search or sign up with an alumni reunion site such as Classmates.com (*www.classmates.com*) or Reunions.com (*www.reunions.com*). Adoption search is a bit beyond the scope of this book, but if you're looking for a birth parent or child, there are many online resources to assist you — enter *adoption search* or *adoption reunion* in your favorite search engine.

Search Tools and Strategies

The hallmark of a good online genealogist is knowing how to work the search engines or databases to find what he seeks. But knowing *how* to search is not enough by itself. You also need to know where to search, and what to do with the results. To help you with this, several search tools and strategies are outlined below.

Bring Back Sites from the Dead

How many times have you found a link to a promising Web site, only to find that it leads to a File Not Found page? Web sites are in a state of constant flux, with webmasters changing file names, switching ISPs, or just taking down the site or letting the domain name lapse because they no longer have the time or interest to maintain it. As frustrating as this is, a File Not Found, or 404, error does not always mean the content is gone forever.

- **Trim back the URL.** Perhaps someone just moved that particular page into a new folder, or otherwise rearranged or renamed some of the files on the site. Try trimming the URL of the page you're trying to access back to the root domain (the root domain being everything between the http:// and the next backslash) to see if the site exists. If it does, use the Search feature or click on likely links or tabs to find the page you want.

- **Try Google Cache.** When you follow a link from Google that comes up 404, or missing, hit the Back button to return to Google and click on the little Cached link at the end of the Google listing for the site. This will bring up a copy of the page as it appeared at the time that Google last indexed the page.

- **Visit the Internet Archive.** Sometimes sites really are taken offline. Even that doesn't mean the information is necessarily lost forever. The Wayback Machine at Internet Archive preserves Web sites for posterity by taking regular "snapshots" of Web pages at various points in time. Type a URL into the Wayback Machine search box (*www.archive.org*), then select a date from the available archives and you can begin surfing an archived version of the Web page.

Use the Find Feature in Your Browser

Many genealogy transcriptions and records appear online as long scrolling pages of text. To quickly search these pages for a particular name or other piece of information, use the Find feature in your browser. To access the Find feature, press CTRL+F for PCs, or the COMMAND+F for Macs.

Search the Web with a Toolbar

Many genealogists are fans of the Google Toolbar because it allows them to access all of the advanced search features of Google without having to take the extra step of visiting the Google home page. The built-in pop-up blocker helps cut down on annoying ads. You can translate pages into English instantly with just one click. And, best of all, the terms you search for appear as clickable links in the toolbar. Just click on one and Google takes you right to the first place on the page where that search term appears (just like the browser Find feature discussed above). Other search engines also offer integrated toolbars. About.com Web Search Guide Wendy Boswell offers links to some of the best at Best Toolbars on the Web (*http://websearch.about.com/od/dailywebsearchtips/qt/dnt0418.htm*).

Use the Steve Morse One-Step Search Tools

The One-Step search pages (*www.stevemorse.org*) created by Steve Morse offer enhanced search options for popular genealogical databases such as Ellis Island Records, Ancestry.com, and the Social Security Death Index. In almost every case, the One-Step search offers more flexibility than the original database's search engine. Use these one-step tools as a back door when you're unsuccessful at searching popular databases directly.

E-LINK

For further help with understanding and using search engines to effectively find what you need, check out the Spider's Apprentice *(www.monash.com/spidap.html)*. The site rates the various search engines based on their effectiveness, offers a variety of search strategies for finding various types of information on the Web, and also explains how to improve your own search-engine ranking if you maintain a blog or Web site.

Find the Right Tree in the Forest

Individuals are unique. Names are not. When searching for your ancestors on the Internet, you'll quickly find that there are numerous people with the same name. Even unusual names may not be as uncommon as you think. Dempsey and Kinchen Owens may sound like unusual names, but there were actually several men sporting those monikers living in mid-nineteenth-century North Carolina!

To avoid the pitfall of merging two people with the same name into one, certified genealogist Marsha Hoffman Rising, author of *The Family Tree Problem Solver*, always assumes that two people of the same name lived in the same community. This reminds you not to attach a piece of data to a specific individual until you're sure that you have the right person. Search for *all* available records, and use them to identify the distinguishing characteristics of your ancestor. Two men with the same name will have different wives, different children, and perhaps a different occupation. Most importantly, they won't usually occupy the same piece of property, so be sure to include land and property records in your search.

ALERT!

One popular method for locating ancestors with common surnames such as Smith or Powell is to search for other less common names from your ancestor's family. If your John Smith has a son named Elias, try searching for Elias Smith. Also look for sisters who married men with more unusual names.

It's not unusual to find two men of the same name living in the same community identified as Sr. and Jr. in local records, causing many researchers to mistakenly connect them as father and son. In reality, they could have a different family relationship, such as uncle and nephew, or even no relationship at all — with *junior* and *senior* used solely to distinguish between an elder and a younger man with the same name. These and other relationship terms such as *aunt* and *cousin* were often used very loosely in earlier times — and still are, even today. The lesson? It's important not to jump to hasty conclusions. Take time to research multiple sources of information for each individual and event in your family tree so you can be sure you have the correct individual identified as your ancestor.

CHAPTER 4: Online Starting Points

The Internet is overflowing with tens of thousands of sites with family history information. With just a few clicks of your mouse, you can learn how to get started researching your family history, explore historical databases for your ancestors, share your discoveries with family and friends, and network with other genealogists. It's exciting and addicting, but without a road map, you may quickly find yourself lost.

What Is and Is Not Online

To help acquaint you with genealogy research online, this chapter presents some of the largest and most popular online sites to begin your family history search. Most of these will include sources in the form of indexes, transcriptions and abstracts, or digital images.

- **Indexes** — An index is a list of names, possibly including other relevant details such as date or location of an event, that directs you to the original documents in which the names appear.

- **Transcriptions and abstracts** — In a transcription, the full text of a document is copied out and placed online as text. Sometimes information is "abstracted," which means that only the most relevant details are pulled out.

- **Images** — The original document is scanned and may be presented online as an image file, a PDF file, or a document that you must view through a special viewer that you'll download to your computer.

Most online data comes in the form of indexes, because they are the least time-consuming and least costly to prepare and place online. This has important implications for genealogists, as it means you cannot do all of your research online. More and more indexes are now being linked to digital scans of the original documents, however. In cases where these scans aren't available online, all information you derive from indexes and transcriptions will have to be checked against the original source — often necessitating a letter, call, or visit to a courthouse, archives, or other records repository.

Explore Free Databases

Thanks to the efforts of hundreds of thousands of volunteer genealogists and historians, there is a wealth of free genealogy data available online. Government agencies, libraries, and archives have also jumped on the digital bandwagon, offering free Internet access to some of the many public records under their domain. Most of these free databases of interest to genealogists will be introduced in the chapters where they are most relevant. The Ellis Island database, for example, will be discussed in Chapter 10. Here, however, you'll learn about some of the largest generalpurpose sites for free genealogy research.

Root Around at RootsWeb

The oldest and largest free community genealogy site on the Web, Roots Web (*www.rootsweb.com*) offers hundreds of gigabytes of free genealogy data, including more than 8 million records contributed by users. Search tabs at the top lead you to some of RootsWeb's most popular features:

- Click on Searches to access a variety of search engines and indexes. Here you'll find the RootsWeb Surname List (RSL), a list or registry of surnames along with information about how to contact the person who submitted the surname so you can share information and compare notes. This is also where you'll find links to the RootsWeb-hosted genealogy records and databases, organized by location and/or record type.

- The Family Trees tab takes you to the massive WorldConnect project, a lineage-linked database with more than 460 million names. Learn more about WorldConnect in the "Look in Lineage-Linked Databases" section later in this chapter.

- The next two tabs take you to Mailing Lists and Message Boards, where you can connect with other researchers, ask questions about your family history, or search through over a decade of archived posts. See Chapter 11 for more on these features.

- RootsWeb hosts tens of thousands of Web sites for the genealogy community, including personal sites, surname sites, and major free genealogy projects. This list offers a good jumping-off point for exploring your roots.

Find Local Records at the USGenWeb Project

The goal of this large volunteer genealogy project is to maintain Web sites for genealogical research in every U.S. state and county. The databases, links, and information found at the USGenWeb Project (*www.usgenweb.org*) are all free, but because the sites are all maintained entirely by volunteers, the quality and quantity of the information vary widely from site to site. Whenever you're researching in a new locality, however, it's helpful to begin with a visit to the local GenWeb site to check out the available databases, learn about the area's geography and changing boundaries, and identify local resources for research in the area.

QUESTIONS?

How reliable is the information found in online family history databases?

Much of the genealogy data available online appears in the form of indexes, transcriptions, and abstracts. These derivative sources are generally reliable, but are prone to human error and may not always include everything found in the original source. Look for data with full source information so you can verify the facts you find online against the original record.

Look in Lineage-Linked Databases

Lineage-linked databases offer family historians an easy way to search, contribute, view, or download family trees online. Instead of just a simple list or index of names, lineage-linked databases present family trees in a linked, pedigree format. Because these compiled databases offer access to millions of names and multiple generations of a family tree, they are a favorite of many online genealogists.

The Internet's largest collection of family tree files can be found in the combined Ancestry World Tree/RootsWeb WorldConnect database. The database, containing over 460 million names, can be searched at both Ancestry.com as Ancestry World Tree (*www.ancestry.com/trees/awt/main.aspx*) or at RootsWeb as RootsWeb WorldConnect (*http://worldconnect.rootsweb.com*). Advanced search options, easy submission of your own family tree, contact information for submitters, and the ability to add electronic notes makes this lineage-linked database a favorite with online genealogists. Ancestry.com also offers a separate database of user-submitted family trees with over 500 million names, known as Ancestry Member Trees (*http://trees.ancestry.com*).

Back on the FamilySearch site, the Pedigree Resource File (*www.familysearch.org*) is another good lineage-linked collection of family trees. It includes more than 150 million names and presents the results in familiar family tree format. Unlike the older Ancestral File, Pedigree Resource File includes sections for notes and source documentation, although many submitters do not use this feature.

E-LINK

In addition to the large lineage-linked databases available through Ancestry.com/RootsWeb and FamilySearch, other pedigree sites (some free and some subscription) include GenCircles (*www.gencircles.com*), GeneaNet (*www.geneanet.org*), Kindred Konnections (*www.mytrees.com*), and One Great Family (*www.onegreatfamily.org*).

Despite the convenience of being able to download a big chunk of your family history in one place, lineage-linked or pedigree databases have one huge drawback. They are only as reliable as the researcher or hobbyist who posted them. The first option for evaluating a family tree's reliability is to look for good documentation of sources and conclusions, but to find such welldocumented pedigrees online is rare. To ensure that the information you have found is correct, you'll want to follow up all facts in original sources.

Seek Out Subscription Sites

Commercial sites generally offer the greatest wealth of genealogy data, drawn from records around the world. This information comes with a price tag, however, in the form of subscription or pay-per-view access. When evaluating a commercial genealogy site, consider whether the payment is worth the return in terms of the unique databases or records you will gain access to, or the time you will save by being able to access them from your home.

Ancestry.com

The largest commercial online source for family history information is Ancestry.com (*www.ancestry.com*), a product of the Generations Network. More than 24,000 searchable databases are drawn from census records, immigration records, military records, historical newspaper articles, and birth, marriage, and death records. As a subscriber to Ancestry.com, you can:

- **Search for historical records.** Ancestry.com has more than 5 billion names, pulled together from census records, immigration records, historical newspapers, military records, vital records, and a variety of other resources. Advanced search features allow you to search across all databases at once.

- **View digital images of original records.** Ancestry.com places a focus on scanning and digitizing historical documents for online viewing. This organization's efforts made it the first site online to offer indexes and images of the complete U.S. census, 1790–1930. It also offers digitized passenger lists, British and

Canadian census records, and U.S. military records such as Civil War pension application cards and World War I draft registration cards.

- **Connect with others researching the same ancestors.** The large genealogy community at Ancestry.com offers numerous chances to benefit from the research of others. The majority of the community features at Ancestry.com are free and available to even nonsubscribers, including user-submitted family trees and family history message boards.

Ancestry.com is a subscription-based site, offering unlimited access to records for a monthly or annual fee. At the time of publication this site offers four inclusive subscription packages: U.S. Deluxe, Canada Deluxe, U.K. Deluxe, and World Deluxe. A special subscription version for libraries, called Ancestry Library Edition, may be available to you for free through your local library, but you'll only have access from the library computers. This database is not available for remote access from home with a library card. Ancestry.com also offers free access to patrons at the Family History Library and select larger Family History Centers, through a special arrangement with the Church of Jesus Christ of Latter-day Saints (the LDS or Mormon Church).

Genealogy.com

Just about everything available at Genealogy.com is also available at Ancestry.com, and Ancestry offers better search options. The Generations Network (which owns both sites) is also putting much more emphasis on building up the databases and resources of Ancestry.com. If you're only interested in a particular database, however, Genealogy.com (*www.genealogy.com*) might save you a bit of money. The site still offers subscriptions to some of its individual databases, such as the U.S. Census Collection, while Ancestry.com only offers all-inclusive subscription rates. If you have free use of HeritageQuest Online through your local library, you'll be able to access the same U.S. Census Collection and Family and Local Histories Collection that you'll find at Genealogy.com.

E

Some databases at Ancestry.com and RootsWeb offer a special Post-em Note feature to help you connect with other researchers interested in the same family. This electronic equivalent of a yellow sticky note allows you to attach information such as your name and e-mail address or corrected data to a record. A slightly different version of the feature can be found listed in some Ancestry.com databases as Comments and Corrections.

GenealogyBank

NewsBank offers online access to millions of records from its digital vaults through a service geared specifically to genealogists. Known as Genealogy Bank (*www.genealogybank.com*), the subscription-based product launched in 2006 and offers access to 26 million obituaries from more than 1,000 newspapers, digital images of pages from thousands of family and local history books, over 130,000 historical documents, and a full-text collection of historical newspapers. Unlimited access is available for a monthly or annual subscription, and there is a money-back guarantee if you're not satisfied. A similar service called America's GenealogyBank is available for library subscription, so check with your local or state library before you subscribe. You may already have access to this database through one of these sources.

WorldVitalRecords

Another relative newcomer to online genealogy, WorldVitalRecords (*www.worldvitalrecords.com*), a product of FamilyLink.com, offers both free and paid family history content. The company is headed by former MyFamily.com founder, Paul Allen, and is already well on its way to being a large presence in the world of online genealogy. Most of the free content, including the Social Security Death Index, the Bureau of Land Management Records, World War II Army Enlistment Records, and select state death indexes are also free elsewhere online. Unique content available at WorldVitalRecords includes the SmallTownPapers collection, content from the Everton Genealogical Library, English parish registers, and other genealogical data. World-VitalRecords stands out for its focus on unusual and less-used family history sources from all over the world.

ALERT!

Digital images of original records found online are considered by most genealogists to offer a reasonable substitute for the original record in almost every research situation. In other words, if you've accessed a digital image of a census enumeration or military record from a reputable source, it's generally not necessary to also view the original record.

Family Tree Connection

This relatively inexpensive subscription-based site specializes in unique records of interest for family history. Databases available at Family Tree Connection (*www.familytreeconnection.com*) include school yearbooks, association membership rosters, orphanage records, church records, donation lists, and insurance claims. Most of the information spans 1830 to 1930 and comes from U.S. sources.

Find Family at FamilySearch

The Family History Library (FHL) in Salt Lake City has the largest collection of genealogical materials in the world, thanks to the diligent work of members of the Church of Jesus Christ of Latter-day Saints. Their online presence at FamilySearch (*www.familysearch.org*) features nearly a billion names in searchable databases — all of them free.

At the time of this writing, a new version of FamilySearch is in beta testing and available only to church members in select temple districts. Dubbed the "New FamilySearch," the Web site will incorporate a unified Family-Search Family Tree for uploading, recording, and browsing family trees; Record Search for searching digitized genealogical records and transcriptions; and other interactive research features. New features will be added to or linked to from the FamilySearch site at *www.familysearch.org* as they become ready for primetime. You can keep up with current beta projects and changes in the FamilySearch Lab (*http://labs.familysearch.org*).

ESSENTIALS

FamilySearch is in the process of digitizing the millions of rolls of micro-filmed records preserved in its Granite Mountain Records Vault, for free online access to the public. In addition, they are partnering with other entities, such as the National Archives, to digitally capture, preserve, and publish other important genealogical records online. Many of these digital documents and indexes have already been added to the free Family Search Record Search, currently available at *http://pilot.familysearch.org*.

Just Enter a Name

A variety of free online databases are available for searching on FamilySearch. You can either just enter a name from the Home Page, or click on Advanced Search for more search options and a list of individual databases.

- **Census Transcriptions and Indexes** — Search the census index to find ancestors in the 1880 U.S. Federal Census (50 million names), the 1881 Census of Canada (4.3 million names), or the 1881 Census of England and Wales (25 million names). From the search results page, click on a name to view the individual record. From that page, don't miss the Household link in the upper right corner to access a list of all individuals in the household.

- **International Genealogical Index** — More than 285 million baptisms and marriages from around the world can be found in this database, along with a few births and burials. Many of these events were extracted from original records, while others were submitted by members of the church. Click on the Source Call No. link from the IGI individual record page to learn the source of any data you find.

- **Ancestral File and Pedigree Resource File** — Both of these lineage-linked databases include family trees submitted by family historians worldwide. Ancestral File is the older of the two, and doesn't always provide details on the original source of the data. Pedigree Resource File is a more recent incarnation that offers notes and source documentation.

- **Vital Records Index** — The church is in the process of indexing vital records from around the world. Currently vital records for Mexico and Scandinavia are available for online searching.

Make Use of the Family History Library Catalog

For a small fee, almost every microfilm in the vast Family History Library collection can be borrowed through your local Family History Center. While you won't be able to borrow or view the films online (at least not yet), you can use the Family History Library Catalog (FHLC) to view available records and plan your research strategy. This virtual catalog to the vast holdings of the Family History Library can be searched by place, surname, author, subject, call number, or film/fiche number.

- Use **Place Search** to find catalog entries of records from a particular town, county, state, or country.

- Use **Surname Search** to find catalog entries about records that include a specific surname. This search is for locating written family histories, and will not return family names found in microfilmed records such as births, census records, land records, wills, etc.

- Use **Author Search** to find catalog entries by or about a person, church, society, or government agency.

- Use **Title Search** if you know the exact name of the book or film you're looking for.

- Use **Call Number Search** to find catalog entries by the call number used to locate books and other items on the Family History Library's shelves.

- Use the **Film/Fiche Search** to find the contents of a specific microfilm or microfiche.

The most useful search for most genealogy purposes is Place Search because it will return a list of all available records from the area where your ancestor lived that have been filmed by the church.

ALERT!

The LDS Church operates over 4,000 Family History Centers (FHC) in more than eighty countries around the world. These branch facilities of the Family History Library in Salt Lake City offer access to the library's vast genealogical holdings, through electronic databases and microfilm loan. While these centers are usually located inside buildings belonging to the church, everyone is welcome regardless of their religious beliefs. Visit (*www.familysearch.org/Eng/Library/FHC/frameset_fhc.asp*) to find a Family History Center near you.

Borrow Microfilm

Once you find a record of interest in the FHLC, click on View Film Notes to locate call numbers for microfilms that contain the record you seek. With the name of the record and the call number for the film, you can submit a loan request through your local Family History Center. They charge a small fee of a few dollars per microfilm to cover shipping and handling to and from the Family History Library in Salt Lake City. Most films will be available for viewing at your local FHC within a few weeks of your order. Books are generally not available for loan.

Even if you don't plan to borrow microfilms, the FHLC is a great way to view the types of records that are available for your locality and time period of interest. A place search in the catalog for *Edgecombe County, North Carolina*, for example, displays a wide variety of records, from bible records to voting registers. By selecting Land Records from the list, you learn that the county maintains deed records from 1732 to 1931, and an index to the deeds from 1759 to 1920.

Access Helpful Research Tools and Guidance

Another thing that FamilySearch does well is teach newcomers about genealogy. Under the Search tab, select the Research Helps link to view Research Outlines for various states and countries, free genealogy worksheets and charts, letter-writing guides, and foreign genealogy word lists.

Discover History at the National Archives

The U.S. National Archives and Records Administration (NARA) preserves a huge amount of information related to the history of our nation and its people — the paper documents alone would circle the earth over fiftyseven times if laid end to end! Because the records at the National Archives (*www.archives.gov*) come from every branch of the federal government, almost all Americans can find themselves, their ancestors, or their community in the archival holdings.

The cost to digitize such a huge volume of materials is prohibitive, so only a small percentage of the National Archives records are available for research online. Instead, the greatest value of the site is in its research tools, such as microfilm indexes and finding aids, and articles on various record types and how to access them. There are, however a few exceptions, such as Casualty Lists for the Korean and Vietnam Wars, and Selected Chinese Exclusion Lists. Most of the rest of the available data on their Web site can be accessed through one of two NARA search engines.

- The **Archival Research Catalog (ARC)** (*www.archives.gov/research/arc*) is the online catalog of NARA and currently describes about 50 percent of its holdings. In some cases ARC will take you directly to an online record or database. You can search ARC by keyword, location, organization, person, or topic. You can also restrict your search to return digitized images only, which will include photographs as well as digitized copies of original documents. Useful genealogy databases that can be accessed through ARC include World War II Casualty Lists; indexes to several Native American census rolls, including the Guion-Miller Roll and Dawes Rolls; and fugitive slave case papers and petitions.

- The **Access to Archival Databases (AAD)** (*http://aad.archives.gov/aad*) allows you to search for free through over 85 million documents, including passenger lists for people who fled the Irish famine for the United States in the 1840s, photos of natural and manmade disasters, and the popular World War II army enlistment file. Be sure to check out the Search Values feature for any search field you use. In the World War II file, for example, you need to enter names as lastname, firstname (*owens, james*) and the year of birth as a twodigit number (such as *23*).

The National Archives has partnered with Footnote to digitize additional records from its vast holdings. Over 23 million pages have been digitized so far. While access to the digitized materials will be available for no charge in the National Archives facilities, these records are only available online on a subscription basis. The agreement does, however, state that these digitized images will be available at no charge on the National Archives Web site as well, after an interval of five years. National Archives content that is currently available on Footnote (*www.footnote.com*) includes records of the Southern Claims Commission, a name index to Civil War and later pension files, Revolutionary War documents, naturalization records for several states, Civil War confederate service records, FBI files, and the Mathew B. Brady collection of Civil War photographs.

Look at the Library of Congress

While many may not classify the Library of Congress (*www.loc.gov*) as a starting point for online genealogy research, it has a number of important features and collections that warrant its inclusion in this chapter.

As mentioned in Chapter 2, the Library of Congress Online Catalog (*http://catalog.loc.gov*) is one of the best places to search online for published local and family histories. While the books themselves are not available online, you can easily see what books have been published that may relate to your research. With this information you can try contacting local libraries or historical societies to see if they have a copy of this book you can borrow, or have them make copies of the pages that concern your ancestors.

The American Memory Collection (*http://memory.loc.gov*) presents a digital record of American history, chronicling historic events, people, places, and ideas through documents, maps, sheet music, moving images, sound recordings, and oral histories. Enter your family name or hometown in the search box available at the top of each page to see if information about your ancestors or the community in which they lived is included in the online American Memory collection.

Search State Libraries and Archives

The state library or archive can often be a genealogist's best friend — even online genealogists. Many are scanning, digitizing, and indexing the most popular records from their vast holdings, and placing them online for free access by genealogists, historians, and other researchers. Budget shortages and other issues may dictate that new data isn't added as quickly as everyone might like, but these state resources often offer access to databases or indexes not available elsewhere online.

ESSENTIALS

Not all major libraries and archives yet offer online access to public records, but most maintain an online catalog of their holdings. Many will also allow you to request copies of records online. Some, such as the North Carolina State Archives, charge out-of-state residents a special handling fee for this service.

The Illinois State Archives, one of the first to provide online access to selected records, offers a Statewide Marriage Index, 1763–1900, and a Statewide Death Index, 1917–1950, along with public-domain land sales, emancipation records, military records, and several county-level probate and circuit court indexes. Another good example is the Missouri State Archives, where you can search a database of births and deaths prior to 1910, or search and view digital copies of death certificates from 1910 to 1956. For those researching in Virginia, the Web site of the Library of Virginia offers a wealth of genealogy data including World War I History Questionnaires, historical Virginia photographs, and a database of Virginia Land Office patents, grants, and surveys from 1623 to 1992. Try a search for *"your state name" archives* or *"your state name" state library* to locate such sites.

CHAPTER 5: Dig into Death Records

Since genealogy research begins with the present before moving back into the past, death records are a good place to begin your search. They often provide enough detail to help verify that you have the correct individual, and may include facts that you don't already have to help you reach back to the previous generation. Death records are also some of the easiest records to find online, because of concerns over online privacy for living individuals.

A Good Place to Begin

Why should you care when your grandfather died when what you really want to know is who your great-grandparents are? Death records — including death certificates, tombstone inscriptions, obituaries, and funeral home records — all provide important clues to an individual's past. Your grandfather's death certificate may list the maiden name of his mother, a significant little tidbit that living family members no longer recall. His obituary may mention a surviving sister, the great-aunt that you never knew existed. His tombstone may tell you that he was a member of the Sons of Confederate Veterans. Records from the funeral home may indicate his exact date of birth.

A second, but equally important, reason for beginning a search with death records is that they are among the most easily accessible records. The fact that the individual is deceased makes privacy less of a concern. Now all of this is not to say that you should always begin a genealogy search with death records. There's nothing wrong with beginning with your grand-parents' marriage record, or their enumeration in the 1930 U.S. census. But once you've gathered as much information as you can from family members, death records generally make sense as the next good place to take your family history quest.

Search for Obituaries

Whenever you embark on a new family history project, it is often helpful to begin by searching for an obituary. This not only helps confirm the individual's date of death, but often provides extra family details that you may not have — the names of extended family members, place of birth, occupation, religious faith and/or place of worship, organization memberships, and any other particulars that people felt were important enough to mention in summing up the life of the deceased.

Biographies of soul singer James Brown repeatedly mention his being raised by his great-aunt Hansone Washington for a time, but offer few clues as to exactly how she was related. Was she a great-aunt on the mother's side or father's side? Was she an aunt or a great-aunt (the biographies don't agree)? Who were her parents? An online obituary for Mrs. Hansone Washington in the *Augusta Chronicle*, dated Saturday, June 18, 1977, provides some insight:

> *Mrs. Hansone Washington, 1029 Bennett Lane died Thursday in an Augusta hospital. Funeral arrangements will be announced by Blount Funeral Home. Survivors include two sisters, Mrs. Josephine Gilliam and Mrs. I. Ganes; two brothers, Mansfield Scott and Willard Scott; and five sons, Stanley E. Figenson, Mike Jowery, Ella Figenson, William Glen, and Johney Washington. Friends may call at the residence or at Blount Funeral Home.*

Armed with the names of her brothers and sisters from this obituary, you can identify the family of Hansone ("Handsome") Scott in the 1910 census of Barnwell County, S.C., prior to her marriage to William Washington and move to Augusta, Georgia. Obituaries from other family members, including the father of James Brown, help clarify her relationship to the singer.

When searching for an obituary, be sure to investigate all of the likely newspapers. Many cities have more than one paper, and an obituary for a specific individual could appear in more than one place. A thorough search should include the city where the person died and any locations where they lived for many years or still have family. You never know which paper is going to have the most detailed obituary, or turn up the one important clue that is omitted from the rest. Check the papers for at least a week after the individual's death. Often a brief obituary or death notice will appear in the first day or two after the death and a longer, full obituary will follow a day or two later.

Obituaries of the past are often not as lengthy and detailed as more modern obituaries. Many of them are little more than a brief notice of the death and funeral arrangements. More recent obituaries are also much easier to locate online, while one from twenty or more years ago may require microfilm research or a request to the newspaper in which it was published. But for a genealogist some information is better than no information at all, so don't assume that obituaries are only useful for people who died within the past few decades.

Look Online

There are many sources for locating obituaries online, such as major historical databases, volunteer obituary transcription sites, and the Web site of the newspaper itself. Google Archive Search (*http://news.google.com/archivesearch*) provides an easy way to search over 200 years of archived news content from individual publishers and news aggregators, making it a good place to begin your search. Both free and fee-based content is included in Archive Search. Search results available for a fee are clearly labeled as "pay-per-view" or list a specific fee to access the content. Links from Google take you directly to the Web site of the publisher or aggregator where the content is hosted. When there are more than just a handful of results, a useful timeline will appear in the left-hand navigation with links to help you drill down into search results by decade or year. None of this is content you can't find through searching directly on the publishers' Web sites, but Google's service makes it easy to search and navigate through multiple sources at once. If you end up with too many results for the individual's name, try adding search terms such as *obituary*, *funeral*, or *died* to help focus your results.

> Searches for obituaries in Google Archive Search often yield results from the NewsBank service with a per-article access fee that varies by publisher. If you think you'll need to look at more than one or two articles or obituaries, you may get a better value through GenealogyBank *(www.genealogybank.com)*. Their America's Obituaries collection contains over 26 million obituaries from NewsBank, dating from 1977 to the present.

A variety of specialized search services can also help you locate an obituary online. The Obituary Daily Times (*www.rootsweb.com/~obituary*) offers a daily index of published obituaries compiled by volunteers and distributed freely via e-mail list. The entire database going back to about 1999 is also searchable online. The Obituary Daily Times does not index all published obituaries, just the ones selected for inclusion by the volunteers. It also does not have the actual newspaper notices, just the name of the deceased, and the publication and date where the obituary appeared. ith this information you can then request a copy of the obituary from the library or directly from the newspaper. ObitFinder (www.obitfinder.com) from Legacy.com links to online obituaries from U.S. and Canadian newspapers.

Some require a fee to access. Obituary Central (www.obitcentral.com) organizes links by state and county to transcribed funeral notices and obituaries appearing on various genealogy Web sites going back to about 1998. It also links directly to search results for death notices on newspaper Web sites. Subscription-based obituary and newspaper search sites such as ObitsArchive.com, NewspaperARCHIVE.com, and the National Obituary Archive (www.arrangeonline.com) can also be useful in locating obituaries. Many general genealogy subscription sites also get into the act; Ancestry.com, Footnote.com, and World Vital Records (www.worldvitalrecords.com), for example, all offer online obituary and/or historic newspaper collections.

Locate Newspaper Web Sites

Use your favorite search engine to locate newspapers published in the area where your ancestor lived or died. A search for the town or county name and *newspaper* will usually turn up what you need. If you know the newspaper's title, you can search for that directly. Once you find the newspaper's Web site, visit the Obituaries section to see how far back in time these go. Look for an Archives section as well, where the newspaper offers access to older material. Some newspapers leave obituaries online forever, some for a year, some for just a week or two. Some may charge for access to older articles and obituaries.

Look for a Library Web Site

The public library that serves the area in which your ancestor lived or died is often an excellent source for obituary and death notices. Many maintain obituary clipping files or, at the very least, have back issues of area newspapers available on microfilm. Many library Web sites even offer online indexes to obituary notices from their area. From there it often takes no more than an e-mail or quick letter to get a copy of the actual obituary. Many libraries don't even charge for this service or request only minimal reimbursement for copying and postage. If you can't find anything on the Web site, contact the library via phone or e-mail to see how its staff handles such requests. See Chapter 8 for more about locating and using libraries in your genealogy research.

Utilize Your Local Library

Many libraries subscribe to a variety of helpful research databases for free use by their patrons. Subscriptions to databases such as NewsBank, America's GenealogyBank, ProQuest Obituaries, or Ancestry Library Edition can be useful for obituary searches. Contact your local or state library to see what databases are offered (most list them on their Web site) and whether you can connect from home with your library card number.

Social Security Death Index

When you're unsure of an individual's date of death, head straight for the Social Security Death Index (SSDI). This large database compiled by the U.S. Social Security Administration (SSA) contains vital information for more than 80 million people (primarily Americans) whose deaths have been reported to the SSA.

What You Will Find in the SSDI

Once you locate an individual in the Social Security Death Index, you may find some or all of the following information: first and last name, date of death, date of birth, social security number (SSN), the state where the SSN was issued, the last known residence of the deceased, and the location where the last SSA benefit was sent.

What You Won't Find in the SSDI

The biggest mistake that researchers make when using the SSDI is in assuming that it is an index to all deceased individuals who have held social security numbers. That is not the case. It is also not a database of all deceased persons who have received social security benefits, or whose families have received survivor benefits. Instead the SSDI indexes individuals whose deaths were reported to the Social Security Administration, the majority of them after 1962 when SSA first computerized its processing of benefits. If a relative of the deceased or the funeral director did not report the death, or if the individual died prior to 1963, you probably won't find that person's name in the index.

How to Search the SSDI

The complete Social Security Death Index, current up to within the past few months, is available for free searching online on several different Web sites. A few sites require a fee for access, but their offerings are no better than the free versions. A good place to start is the handy search form by Steve Morse titled "Searching the Social Security Death Index in One Step" (*www.stevemorse.org/ssdi/ssdi.html*). It combines all of the desirable search features from the various SSDI Web sites into one easy search. Other free SSDI search options include RootsWeb (*http://ssdi.rootsweb.com*) and New England Ancestors (*www.newenglandancestors.org/research/database/ss*).

Locating a particular individual in this large database, especially if you aren't sure when and where this person died, can be an exercise in frustration. Be sure to take advantage of all the search features available to you, and try different combinations of searches.

- Search by last name or first name only, in combination with other known facts such as date or year of birth and state of last residence. The first name in combination with the exact birth date, or month and year of birth, often produces results.

- Search for women under both their married name and their maiden name.

- Enter an initial in the given name field.

- Omit the zip code because this field does not exist for earlier records.

- Try alternate spellings in the name field, making use of wildcard operators when available (see Chapter 3).

Order a Copy of the Social Security Application

With the name and social security number from the SSDI, you can request a copy of your ancestor's original application for social security, otherwise known as Form SS-5. This form was completed by individuals applying for a social security number and asked for information that is of great value to genealogists, such as parents' names (including the mother's maiden name), date of birth, employer, and, later, the place of birth. The fee to receive the Social

Security Application Form is a bit steep, but well worth it if you don't already know the information that the form often provides. Search online for *ss5 genealogy request* to find information regarding current fees.

The Social Security Administration offers online ordering of photocopies of Social Security Number Application SS-5 forms. A link to the application form with current fees can be found in their Guide to Freedom of Information Act (FOIA) requests (*www.ssa.gov/foia/html/foia_guide.htm*).

Death Certificates and Online Indexes

A death certificate can provide important facts about a person's life — date and cause of death, date and place of birth, parents' names (including mother's maiden name), funeral home, burial location, and name of the informant who provided the information. Since about 1967, most death certificates in the United States also list the deceased's social security number. Actual details included on a death certificate vary from state to state, and by time period.

E-LINK

Vitalrec.com *(www.vitalrec.com)* offers current information for each U.S. state on the availability of death records, instructions and fees for ordering a death certificate copy, and a link to the state department that handles vital records. If you're in a hurry, VitalChek *(www.vitalchek.com)* processes online rush orders for each state, including online credit card payment — for an extra fee, of course.

Death certificates in the United States are primarily a twentieth-century innovation. Most states did not officially register deaths until after 1900; some, such as Georgia and New Mexico, began as late as 1919! There are a few exceptions, namely in New York, New Jersey, and the New England states, where recording of deaths began in the mid-to late 1800s. In the United States, death certificates are generally maintained at the state level, usually through the Department of Health or Vital Records.

Privacy laws may restrict access to death certificates for a certain period of time after the individual's death. A term of fifty years isn't all that uncommon. Some agencies will allow anyone to request a copy of a death certificate, but will black out certain more private information such as the cause of death or social security number unless you are a direct relative of the deceased. When requesting a death certificate from a vital records agency, be prepared to identify your relationship with the deceased and to provide a copy of a valid ID.

Death indexes are available online for many states, counties, and locations. Check first on the Web site of the state vital records office, state archives, and state library. The Ohio Historical Society, for example, includes an online Ohio Death Certificate Index, 1913–1944. The Illinois State Archives hosts the Illinois Statewide Death Index, 1913–1950. At the Minnesota State Archives Web site you can search an index for death certificates from 1908 to 2001. Genealogist Joe Beine organizes links to these and many other online death indexes at Online Searchable Death Indexes and Records (*www.deathindexes.com*).

Ancestry.com offers access to a wide variety of death indexes to its subscribers. Some of these are also available elsewhere on the Web, and some are exclusive online to Ancestry.com. Death indexes can also be found on a variety of other genealogy sites, both free and fee-based. The state and county sites at USGenWeb (www.usgenweb.org) are a good place to find death record transcriptions and indexes, as well as links to offsite indexes. Genealogical society Web sites are another good place to try. Both the Italian Genealogical Group (www.italiangen.org) and German Genealogy Group (www.germangenealogygroup.com), for example, offer online searching of the New York City Death Index, 1891–1948. When all else fails, try a search for *"death index"* and the state name, such as *pennsylvania "death index,"* in your favorite search engine.

One last important online source for death information is the International Genealogical Index (IGI) at FamilySearch (www.familysearch.org). This free database contains millions of birth, marriage, and death dates and places for deceased people from countries around the world. As previously discussed in Chapter 4, the IGI contains information both drawn from extracted vital records and supplied by members of the LDS Church. Remember to check the source information to see where the dates you've found were obtained, and verify them with other sources whenever possible.

Visit Virtual Cemeteries and Funeral Homes

Cemetery tombstones or grave markers are good sources for death information, as well as providing evidence for date of birth, family relationships, military service, and membership in fraternal organizations or societies. Thus, a visit to the cemetery is a must for most family tree projects. Such a visit is not always easily done in person, however. While it can't quite match the special feeling you get standing before your ancestor's tombstone, online research in the form of tombstone transcriptions and photographs affords the opportunity for "virtually" traipsing through cemeteries around the world from the comfort of home.

ALERT!

Tombstones often show the age of the individual when she died in place of either the date of birth or death. If this information is provided in the form years, months, days, such as "Age 22 Years 11 Months and 26 Days," then you can easily calculate the missing date with the help of a birth date calculator (just type birth date calculator into your favorite search engine).

Virtual Cemeteries Have Their Shortcomings

Convenient as it is to research cemetery records online, there are a few disadvantages over a firsthand visit to the cemetery. Keep these in mind as you explore cemetery information online:

- Tombstone information may not always be read and transcribed correctly. Some grave markers can be very hard to read, or the transcriber may have mistyped the information when putting it online. He may also have missed information inscribed on the back of the stone (although the thorough ones won't).

- The arrangement of graves in the cemetery can be important because family members are often buried together or close to one another. That arrangement is not always preserved in the alphabetical listings we sometimes find online. Check to see if some type of placement information has also been transcribed, such as the cemetery section and row. This can at least help identify people buried in the same general area of the cemetery. If the site also includes individual tombstone photos, you can sometimes find clues in them to help identify a gravestone's relative position in the cemetery.

ESSENTIALS

The symbols and architecture you encounter in the cemetery can tell you a lot about your ancestors. *Stories in Stone* by Douglas Keister details many examples of funerary architecture and tombstone symbols, accompanied by photos. Alternatively, look online for information by searching for phrases such as *tombstone symbols* or *cemetery symbolism*.

Find Online Cemetery Databases and Lists

Genealogical societies and volunteers are the greatest source for online cemetery transcriptions, so a good place to begin is on the Web site of an area genealogical society or the appropriate county site at USGenWeb. If that doesn't pan out, use a search engine to locate online cemeteries or transcriptions by entering a phrase such as *greene county virginia cemetery*. Or visit ePodunk (*www.epodunk.com*) or the Geographic Names Information System (*http://geonames.usgs.gov*) to find the names of cemeteries in a given town or county and then search for the cemeteries directly by name. These sites won't usually pick up small family cemeteries, but they at least offer a place to start.

In an effort to preserve the valuable information crumbling away in cemeteries, and to improve access to this information for genealogists, a variety of groups and organizations are collaborating to put cemetery data online. Best of all, these databases are all free!

- **Find a Grave** — Visit the well-organized Find a Grave site (*www.findagrave.com*) to search over 14 million grave records for both the famous and the "nonfamous."

- **Interment.net** — Almost 4 million cemetery records are available for searching or browsing on Interment.net (*www.interment.net*), representing over 8,000 cemeteries around the world.

- **USGenWeb Tombstone Transcription Project** — Browse by state and county to view hundreds of thousands of cemetery transcriptions and photos contributed by volunteers to this special project at USGenWeb (*www.rootsweb.com/~cemetery/photo.html*).

- **JewishGen Online Worldwide Burial Registry** — Well over a halfmillion names are available for searching in this database of Jewish interments in cemeteries and other burial sites worldwide (*www.jewishgen.org/databases/cemetery*).

- **Veterans Affairs Nationwide Gravesite Locator** — Search for burial locations of veterans with the help of the U.S. Department of Veterans Affairs (*http://gravelocator.cem.va.gov*). The site includes information on veterans and their family members buried in veterans and military cemeteries, as well as those buried in private cemeteries where the grave is marked with a government grave marker.

Don't Disregard Funeral Home Records

Genealogists often overlook the records maintained by funeral homes. These can be a very valuable source of family history information. Depending on state or local laws, the funeral director may be the one responsible for filing the death certificate and placing the obituary with the news media, which means all of those valuable details collected from family members may reside in his files. A funeral home file may provide the deceased's date and place of birth, maiden name if a female, date and place of death, burial location, parents' names, veteran status, social security number, and, some-times, names of surviving relatives.

It is important to realize, however, that a funeral home is a private business. Its primary responsibility is to the deceased and the grieving family, not to genealogists. You may find the funeral home to be reluctant about releasing private records. You may also find that older records are stored away in boxes in a basement or attic, or have been thrown out to make room for more current records.

Some funeral home records may be found online in the form of transcribed data. These are generally posted by genealogical societies or volunteers, not the funeral homes. There are exceptions, however. The records of the J.F. Bell Funeral Home in Charlottesville prior to 1970 have been placed online (*www.virginia.edu/woodson/projects/bell/intro.html*) in a collaboration between the funeral home and the African American Genealogy Group of Charlottesville. To find funeral home records in your area of interest, do a search for *funeral records* and the location you are searching — e.g., *funeral records missouri*. You can also use the Internet to locate funeral homes in the area in which you're researching, using an online funeral home directory such as FuneralNet (*www.funeralnet.com*).

ALERT!

Don't believe everything you see on a cemetery tombstone — even if it is carved in stone! This applies to funeral home records, death certificates, and other death records as well. The information is only as reliable as the person who provided it.

If you're unable to find any funeral home data online, you may want to try contacting the funeral home directly. For best results when contacting a funeral home for records, address a written request to the manager of the funeral home. This gives them the opportunity to respond at their convenience. Be specific about what you're looking for, enclose a self-addressed stamped envelope, and offer to pay for any copying expenses.

Put It into Practice

As previously discussed, most Internet searches for family information should generally begin with death records. If you know the date of death, look first for an obituary. If you're not sure of at least the year of death, and your subject died after 1962, begin with the Social Security Death Index. The order doesn't really matter too much, as you should eventually end up scouring all relevant sources of death information, just to make sure you don't overlook anything important.

You have probably heard of Laura Ingalls Wilder, author of the famous *Little House on the Prairie* series. Since she's famous, you can find much more information about her online than you would for most people. Just ignore those biographies and other data for now, however, and search for her obituary using her name and year of death. Because it's free and indexes multiple newspaper databases, Google News Archive Search (*http://news.google.com/archivesearch*) is a good place to begin. A search for *laura ingalls wilder 1957* turns up multiple articles on Mrs. Wilder, but since you're looking for her obituary, click on the date 1957 from the left-hand timeline to narrow the results to articles that appeared the year that she died. This turns up about a dozen results, including several obituary notices — one from the *New York Times* and several from newspapers published in NewspaperARCHIVE, both of which are avail-able only to subscribers.

If you subscribe to either news service, or have access through your local library, you'll be able to read the full obituary that includes a photograph, and information on her life including her work as a writer and editor. It also includes some family facts such as the full married name of her daughter, along with the name of her husband (Almanzo J. Wilder) and the year of their marriage and his death. There are also a few brief mentions of places that she lived — she was born in Wisconsin; she and her husband lived in De Smet, South Dakota, when their daughter was born; they then moved to Florida, and later to the Ozarks. Assuming that you knew little about Mrs. Wilder, this gives you approximate time frames, locations, and names of other family members, which will allow you to search for her in the census and other records.

The obituary also mentioned that Laura Ingalls Wilder died on her family farm, and a quick Internet search can tell you that this was Rocky Ridge Farm, in the Ozarks of Missouri. The next obvious step would be to use this information to locate a death certificate. The Missouri State Archives (*www.sos.mo.gov/archives*) has death records online, but if you weren't aware of this you would search for such a database using the search techniques and resources discussed in this chapter. The downside is that the Missouri Death Certificates database at the state archives presently only covers the years 1910 to 1956, so you can't access the death certificate for Laura Wilder online.

A search of the database does turn up the death certificate for her husband, however, listed as Almanso James Wilder (see pages 80-81). An image of the actual death certificate can be viewed online, and from this you can learn that he died at 7:30 A.M. on 23 October 1949 of "valvular insufficiency," with a secondary cause of "senile" (old age). You'll also learn that Almanzo was born 13 February 1857 in Malone, New York, to James Wilder and Angeline Day; was a retired farmer; and lived about a mile east of the town of Mansfield in Wright County, Missouri. He is listed as having being buried in the Mansfield Cemetery in Mansfield on 28 October 1949. Laura is listed as the informant on the death certificate. The death certificate for Laura Ingalls Wilder will likely have been added to this growing database by the time you read this, but if not, you could order her death certificate through the Department of Vital Records. Information on how to do this is also available online.

There is a lot of vital information on the death certificate that can lead you to additional records and the next generation of Almanzo's family tree. But assuming that Laura is probably buried with her husband, the next step is to search online for information on Mansfield Cemetery. A Google search for *"mansfield cemetery" missouri* turns up a result from the Cemetery Project (*www.thecemeteryproject.com*). Clicking on this link leads us to photos of the cemetery and the Wilder grave.

Granted, Laura and Almanzo are well-known and there is more information available online for them than for most people because the family tree has already been well-researched. Obituaries can be found online for millions of everyday people, however. The Missouri death certificate database where you found Almanzo's death certificate includes everyone who died in Missouri during those years, not just the famous folk. And cemetery transcriptions and other death records are also fairly easy to find online. Just follow these same basic steps with your own ancestors, and you may be surprised at just how much you can find!

RECEIVED NOV 21 1949
District Health Office No. 6,
District File Number 1149-1260
Date Filed 11-28-49

MAR 4 1957

STATEMENT BY LICENSED EMBALMER

I hereby certify that the body whose name is recorded on the reverse side of this certificate was embalmed by me, or by _me_

Student Embalmer No. ....

working under my personal supervision.

Student ....
Student Embalmer

Signed: F. A. Stiffe

Licensed Embalmer No. 3221

P. O. Address Mansfield

Note: The above MUST BE SIGNED BY THE LICENSED EMBALMER in his OWN HANDWRITING. (Failure to comply the above constitutes grounds for revocation of license.)

If this body is not embalmed, fact should be so stated above.

CHAPTER 6: Check the Census

Most people are familiar with the U.S. census, but did you know that federal census enumerators have been going door-to-door asking questions of American families since 1790? While instituted and maintained primarily to track the nation's population for government planning, a census also provides some of the most useful public records for genealogists because it captures detailed information on an individual or family at a particular point in history — essentially a once-per-decade snapshot of the country's inhabitants.

The U.S. Federal Census

Census records are an important tool for family history research. From them you can learn who was living in a household at a particular point in time, including spouses, siblings, and possibly even a mother-in-law. Census records can also tell you the approximate age of the individuals, where they were born, and what they did for a living. Some census records also provide detail on an individual's immigrant status, including the year of immigration and whether the immigrant applied for U.S. citizenship. Best of all, every available U.S. federal census from 1790 to 1930 can be accessed online.

E-LINK

Census extraction forms offer a convenient method for extracting and recording the information that you find as you explore online census records, making it easy to see at a glance what information was collected for a specific census year. Download them for free online from sites such as Ancestry.com (*www.ancestry.com/charts/census.aspx*), About.com Genealogy (*http://genealogy.about.com/od/free_charts/a/us_census.htm*), and CensusTools (*www.censustools.com*).

Exploring the U.S. Federal Census

The United States began to count its citizens in 1790, not long after its birth as a country. This first federal census, instituted by President George Washington, was intended to provide information on residents for the purpose of apportioning members of the House of Representatives and assessing federal tax. Since that first census, the U.S. government has conducted a federal census, or decennial census, once every ten years. However, data from more recent censuses are not available for public inspection because of a seventy-two-year restriction imposed by law to protect the privacy of living individuals. This means the most recent census currently open for public access is 1930 (the 1940 census will be released to the public on April 1, 2012).

Before 1850, census schedules recorded only the name of the head of household and numbers and approximate ages of any other people living in the home. As the country's population grew, the government's need for additional information also grew and new questions were added to the census. The 1850 census is an important census document for researchers, as it was the first census to list names and ages for all individuals in a household, as well as including the place of birth. Another key year is 1880, as it marked the first federal census to document the relationship of household members to the head of household.

In 1900 the census asked for the month as well as year of birth, providing more detailed information on ages than any census before or since. It is also the first available census record to document immigration and citizenship data, asking whether an individual was foreign born, the year of immigration, the number of years in the United States, and the citizenship status of foreign-born individuals over the age of twenty-one. As the twentieth century progressed, additional questions were added to each census, while others were dropped. Most notable: the 1910 census recorded survivors of the Union or Confederate army or navy, the 1920 census asked for the year of naturalization for naturalized citizens, and the 1930 census noted whether the family owned a radio set.

What the Census Can Tell You about Your Ancestors

While the early censuses were little more than a head count of the population, more modern census records are filled with a wealth of valuable data. Most notably, the 1850 to 1930 censuses can provide such details as:

- Names of family members
- Ages for each individual
- State or country of birth
- Parents' birthplaces
- Street address

- Estimated value of their home and personal belongings
- Marriage status and years of marriage
- Occupation
- When they came to the United States and from which country (if applicable)

What you can gain from census records is a wonderful snapshot in time for a particular family or place. You can learn whether your ancestors were literate or spoke English and where they and their parents came from, and even discover neighbors and nearby relatives. By locating your ancestors in multiple census years, you can watch the family grow, and the children move out and start families of their own. You can even use census records to discover whether your ancestors moved, changed jobs, or lost a child.

Access Digital Census Images Online

Traditionally, utilizing census records to research your family tree has involved wading through microfilm copies of the original handwritten pages, produced by the U.S. government to preserve the records from decay. These microfilmed census records are generally available for viewing at Family History Centers, the National Archives, and libraries with a large genealogy or local history section.

E-LINK

The Church of Jesus Christ of Latter-day Saints is in the process of adding free access to indexes and digitized images for U.S. federal and states censuses through RecordSearch, currently located at FamilySearch Labs (*http://pilot.familysearch.org*), but eventually to be part of FamilySearch.org. These indexes are considered by many genealogists to be especially accurate, as the indexing being done by volunteers through FamilySearch Indexing (*www.familysearchindexing.org*), uses a doubleblind data entry method, with discrepancies reviewed and resolved by a third person.

Because census lists were typically recorded in order of visitation, searching for a particular family on a microfilmed record can be cumbersome and time-consuming. The U.S. government did create indexes for many census years to assist researchers in locating specific individuals or families in the microfilmed census records; however, not all census records were indexed, and most were indexed only by the *head of household* — the individual identified to the census taker as the person responsible for the care of the home and/or family. Other members of the same household (with the same surname) are typically not included in a head-of-household index. Thus, even when using a microfilm census index, you may still find it difficult to locate particular individuals without spending hours scrolling page by page and line by line through the microfilm. With the recent advent of everyname computerized indexes, however, knowing the name of your ancestor or relative and the state he or she resided in is often enough to take you directly to the exact page and line where your ancestor is recorded.

In recent years, digitized images of original census pages have revolutionized census research, especially for those researching online. Digitized images take computerized census research up a notch, allowing you to click directly from your search results to a digital copy of the original census page where your ancestors were recorded — in the enumerator's own hand-writing. Digital images are the best census records available online because they allow you to look directly at the record as it was originally created, without having to worry about whether a modern-day transcriber misread the handwriting or mistyped the data. Digital images also allow you to look at *all* of the information included on the original census, while transcriptions usually only include some of the most important details.

This is where Internet genealogy research really provides a boost over more traditional microfilm research. The entire U.S. census, including complete every-name indexes and digital images of the microfilmed pages, is available for searching and viewing on the Internet. Various companies and Web sites offer online access to these digitized census enumerations through a variety of paid subscription options.

Three large subscription-based sites — Ancestry.com, Genealogy.com, and HeritageQuest Online — have the most complete collection of U.S. federal census records available online. Through all three sites you can search census indexes, read transcriptions, and view digital images of the actual census pages.

Ancestry.com

The U.S. Census Collection at Ancestry.com includes every-name indexes and full digital images of every federal census taken in the United States from 1790 to 1930.

- **Pros:** The most complete U.S. census collection available online. Available to anyone with Internet access. Best advanced search options, including wildcard and Soundex search. If your library subscribes to Ancestry Library Edition, you can access the census for free at the library.

- **Cons:** The subscription rate is a bit steep if census records are all you want to access. A census-only subscription is not available. Ancestry Library Edition is not available for remote access, so you'll have to subscribe to Ancestry.com if you want to access their census records from the comfort of home.

The census search options at Ancestry.com offer much greater flexibility than other digital census offerings. You can search by first name, last name, or even a partial name by using the wildcard options. Select the Soundex option in the Spelling drop-down list to search for people with similar-sounding names. Fill in the surname and town, county, or state to find everyone with your surname in that area. Or use the additional search fields such as Age, Birthplace, Race, or Relationship to the Head of Household to help you zero in on the right person. No search field is required, so you can search by just the first name — or without any name at all, using fields such as Age, Location, Sex, Race, or Birthplace to help find someone when nothing else works. Just about the only census search field that Ancestry.com doesn't offer is Occupation — one that would be very useful on occasion!

HeritageQuest Online

Full digital images of every U.S. federal census from 1790 through 1930 are part of the library-based HeritageQuest Online subscription offered through ProQuest. The indexes, created exclusively by HeritageQuest, are more accurate than most, but index the head of household only and are not available for all census years.

- **Pros:** Free to patrons of subscribing libraries. In some cases the images are clearer than other offerings. Good search options, including wildcard search.

- **Cons:** Not all census years are indexed, and the indexes that do exist are head-of-household only so you'll have to look at the actual census images to view details on family members. No Soundex search. Not available for individual subscriptions.

The advanced search screen at HeritageQuest Online offers a decent number of search fields, including Surname, Given Name, Location, Age, Race, and Birthplace. None of the fields are required, so you could, for example, search for all African-Americans living in Aiken County, South Carolina, or for all females named Mandy living in 1880 Chicago.

ALERT!

Free trials, available from most subscription genealogy sites, offer a great way to "try before you buy." Such trial periods are generally short, so make the most of your time by creating a list of the people and records you want to search before you sign up. This will help you better evaluate whether to continue or cancel the subscription.

Genealogy.com

The U.S. Census Collection from Genealogy.com is similar to what you'll find through HeritageQuest Online, because Genealogy.com partnered with ProQuest in 2002. Crisp black-and-white digital images are available for every U.S. federal census from 1790 through 1930, and head-of-household indexes created by either HeritageQuest or Genealogy.com are available for some years.

- **Pros:** A good option if you want a census-only subscription and don't have access to HeritageQuest Online through your local or state library.

- **Cons:** Not all census years are indexed, and those that are include heads of household only. No wildcard or Soundex search — you can't search on anything besides name or location.

Census indexes and images are also available online for other countries, including Canada, England, Scotland, Wales, Ireland, and France. See Chapter 13 for more information and Web sites.

Find Free Census Alternatives

While the major online subscription sites discussed above offer convenient access to the entire U.S. federal census in one place, as well as the greater accuracy of digital images, convenience does come with a price tag. In order to make family history available to all, many individuals and organizations have spent thousands of volunteer hours transcribing census records for their specific locality, ethnic group, or surnames of interest. In some cases, these volunteer census efforts also help fill in gaps not yet covered by the major subscription sites, including state and local censuses conducted in the years between the federal enumerations. This transcribed census data is the next best thing to digital images of the actual census pages and, best of all, can often be accessed for little or no cost.

Check Census Gateway Sites

Census indexes, transcriptions, and abstracts that have been placed online by volunteers and organizations can be most easily found by using a census directory site such as Census Online (*www.census-online.com*). This gateway site has organized links to thousands of free census records from the United States and Canada. Just click on your state of interest, then choose a county to view a list of census records from that area that have been transcribed or digitized. Census Online offers simple, clean navigation and includes the source for each census link. Links to census records at fee-based sites such as Ancestry. com and *Genealogy.com* are also included, but are separated from the free links at the bottom of the page and are clearly marked.

Other good census directories for locating free online census records include:

- **Census Finder** (*www.censusfinder.com*)

- **African American Census Schedules Online** (*www.afrigeneas.com/aacensus*)

View the 1880 U.S. Federal Census at FamilySearch

This comprehensive transcription of the 1880 federal census was created by volunteers from the Church of Jesus Christ of Latter-day Saints over a period of seventeen years and is available for free use on their FamilySearch Web site. Click on the Search tab at FamilySearch (*www.familysearch.org*), and then follow the Census link in the left-hand column to access the database, which includes not only the names of every enumerated individual but also other important details. Soundex search is the default, with a check box to force exact spellings. Once you arrive on an individual result's page, select the Household link to view a transcription of all individuals enumerated in that household. A link is also included to view the original census image on Ancestry.com, but you'll need a subscription.

QUESTIONS?

Which census year should I search first?

It's generally a good idea to begin with the most current census year available and work backward. In most cases, this is the 1930 census. If your ancestor was deceased by 1930, begin your search with the most recent census taken while he was still living, or the most recent census for which you know his location.

Search or Browse the USGenWeb Census Project

Two large volunteer census efforts, both using the USGenWeb name, are outgrowths of the official USGenWeb Project. Neither are formally affiliated with the USGenWeb any longer, although they both still bear its name. Both census projects, however, still display the same volunteer spirit, offering free access to U.S. census data transcribed and put online by volunteers.

The first USGenWeb Census Project (*www.us-census.org*) is hosted online by USGenNet. The navigation is very straightforward, making it easy to see at a glance what census records are available. Select

On-Line Census Inventory to view available census records organized by state, then county. Then use your browser's Find feature to search the page for your names of interest. In some cases a link to a scanned census image is also available. Alternatively, you can use the site's search engine to search across all census records. You can limit your search by state or year.

The second USGenWeb Census Project (*www.usgwcensus.org*) also offers straightforward navigation. Select a state from the right-hand column to view available census transcriptions. The data is displayed in a uniform text format, which can be easily searched by using your browser's Find feature. This site does not link transcriptions to census images.

Access Census Records Online Through Your Local Library

Your library card could be your key to free census access. Hundreds of state, county, and local libraries offer free access to U.S. federal census indexes and images through subscriptions to Ancestry Library Edition or HeritageQuest Online. In the case of HeritageQuest Online, you can even save yourself a trip to the library and access the database remotely from home by logging in with your library card number (sometimes this requires signing up with your library first). Ask your local or state library whether they subscribe to these databases, or check out this fairly comprehensive list from Dick Eastman of libraries offering remote access to HeritageQuest Online (*www.eogen.com/HeritageQuestOnline*).

Census Research Tips and Caveats

Census enumerations are by no means the most reliable of records. At the time the census was recorded, the enumerator may have missed some-one, written a name down wrong, or received inaccurate information. It's not uncommon to find someone who has aged less than five years in the decade between censuses, or whose birthplace changed with each successive decade. Throw in bad handwriting, changing county borders, and missing or illegible records, and there are plenty of opportunities for research frustration.

Because genealogists researching online typically use indexes to locate people in the census, there also exists the extra challenge of dealing with the misinterpretations, typographical errors, and other inaccuracies that often creep in during the census indexing process. This second opportunity for error means that a name could actually have been butchered twice. Perhaps the census taker, tired at the end of a long, hot day, didn't the take time to ask Robert Stuart how his name was spelled, and recorded Stewart instead of Stuart. The individual later responsible for indexing the data was unable to accurately decipher the sloppy handwriting of that tired census taker and interpreted Stewart as Steward. Now, Robert Stuart is Robert Steward and much more difficult to find.

Don't let these caveats scare you away from census records. Census data provides a valuable look at your ancestors in a particular place and time. Census records are also easy to find and use, and can yield a lot of information in a little time. Just keep in mind that census records and indexes are prone to inaccuracy, and the clues found within should always be corroborated with other records when possible.

ALERT!

Old handwriting is often a challenge to read, so it's no wonder census indexes are prone to inaccuracies. The surname CARTER, for example, might have been read as GARTER, or the name CRISP might be spelled as CHRISP or CRIPS. Create a list of alternative spellings for your ancestor's surnames and then try these name variations in every database you search.

Learn Creativity and Patience

When you're having trouble finding your ancestor in the census index, it's time to get creative. Her name may have been misspelled in the census enumeration, or misread when it was indexed. Think about how the name *might* look instead of how it *should* look, considering some of the following suggestions:

- Try alternate spellings for both the first name and last name.

- Search with just a first name and location.

- Don't count solely on Soundex; it doesn't pick up all spelling options for a surname.

- Try a nickname and/or middle name in the first name field.

- Substitute an initial for the first name.

- Search for other family members or even neighbors when you can't find your ancestor.

Expect Little from the 1890 Federal Census

Over 99 percent of the 1890 census population schedules were damaged in a fire, and their remains later destroyed by government order. The few fragments that survive include only about 6,000 names out of an original count of over 62 million. Although most census sites allow you to search the 1890 census, and some have beefed up those names with alternative records from the time period, your chances of finding the person you're looking for are slim.

ESSENTIALS

Special non-population schedules, which include agricultural, manufacturing, and mortality schedules, can be an untapped gold mine for genealogists, providing information on recently deceased individuals and little details of an ancestor's occupation. Other special census enumerations include slave schedules, the 1890 special census of Union Civil War veterans and their widows, and various state and local censuses. Many of these special census enumerations are available online.

Explore the Community

A census enumeration is much more than a record of an individual family. It also tells the story of an entire community. After you get over the excitement of discovering your ancestor, take time to become familiar with the people living nearby. Neighbors could turn out to be related, even if they don't share the same name. It's not uncommon to find a wife's parents living nearby, or an uncle, or married sister. This is especially true in more rural communities. Becoming familiar with the neighbors also allows you to use their names as a search tool to help locate your ancestor in other census records.

Pay Attention to Penmanship

While you're exploring the community, it is also useful to spend time familiarizing yourself with the enumerator's handwriting. Each census taker will have a particular way of styling certain letters, such as a, f, h, j, p, and s. Scan the pages on either side of your ancestor for easily recognizable names to learn how the enumerator wrote certain letters and letter combinations. This will help you to better judge the spelling of your own ancestor's name, as well as those of his family members.

Tax Lists as a Census Alternative

In cases where early census records no longer exist, or when you've misplaced an ancestor between the decennial censuses, tax lists offer a good substitute. Early tax lists generally include all white males over the age of twenty-one, and indicate whether they owned land, slaves, or other taxable property. They usually do not include any other personal information. A Google search for *tax lists genealogy* brings up a wide variety of tax lists online, including 1790/1800 Virginia Tax Lists (*http://homepages.rootsweb.com/~ysbinns/vataxlists*) and 18th Century Tax Lists of Perquimans County, North Carolina (*http://perqtax.homestead.com*).

Go to the Original Record When Possible

Census indexes and transcriptions can provide the information many genealogists want most to find — names, dates, and locations. The original census record, however, will almost always include more. By checking the original census image, you will often discover information that may have been misread or was left out of the transcription. And yes, digitized census images are generally considered an acceptable alternative to the original record.

Use City and County Directories

City and county directories serve as an excellent resource in conjunction with or as an alternative to census records. City directories are much like phone directories, a listing of an area's residents. They differ, however, in that they predate the invention of the telephone and often provide additional information about the listed individuals, such as the street address, place of employment, occupation, or name of spouse. Some also offer a separate street directory, sometimes referred to as a crisscross or reverse directory. This makes it easier to find neighbors, as well as nearby churches, cemeteries, and schools. City directories are compiled through door-to-door surveys and published at irregular intervals. Because they are published based on sales value, they are generally available only for large cities and communities.

City or county directories are especially useful for tracking families between census years, for locating an individual's place of business, and for learning the layout of the area in which your ancestors lived. They aren't always easy to find, however. The Library of Congress (*www.loc.gov/rr/microform/uscity*) has a large collection of U.S. city directories available on microfilm. While they are not available for online perusal or through interlibrary loan, the list of available directories can be browsed for clues to cities and years in which city directories were published. City Directories of the United States of America (*www.uscitydirectories.com*) presents an organized directory of links to city directories that have been microfilmed along with the repositories where the microfilm copies can be accessed. It also includes links to city directory transcriptions that have been made available online. Ancestry.com offers indexes and browsable images of over 1,000 city directories from several U.S. states, primarily in the northeast. Footnote.com also has several early twentieth-and late nineteenth-century city directories from the northeastern United States.

Public libraries often retain copies of city directories published for their area. Check the Web site for libraries in your area of interest to see if they have any city directories available for online browsing. Most won't, but you may be able to e-mail the library to request a lookup.

Put It into Practice

William Rowling, great-great grandfather of Harry Potter author J. K. Rowling, married in England in 1872 at the age of nineteen. His marriage certificate names his father as Edward Rowling. Because the marriage occurred just one year after the 1871 U.K. census, it makes sense to turn directly to census records in order to learn more about William's family. An exact name search for "*edward rowling*" in the 1871 U.K. census at Ancestry.com brings up William's father as the third result — Edward Rowling, born about 1830 in Bassinbourn, Cambridgeshire, England, living with sons William, Henry, and Stephen. Edward is listed as married, but the wife isn't enumerated with them. (More on that in a minute.)

Next, head back one decade to the 1861 U.K. census. Again, the family isn't too difficult to find — but it will take a little more than an exact name search this time. Here the family is enumerated as Rowland, a name they did use for a time. It's close to Rowling, but not similar enough to come up in a Soundex search. A wildcard search for *row** in the last name field does the trick, however, when combined with a few other fields to help narrow down the results (*edward row* born 1830 +/– 2 years in cambridge**). This wildcard trick for first and last names is something to try any time that exact search and Soundex search fail to turn up the expected results. Use of the wildcard for the birth location is also helpful here, covering both Cambridge and Cambridgeshire in one search.

From the 1861 census, you learn that the mother's name is Sarah, born about 1831 in Southampton, Hampshire, England. Since the oldest child, daughter Harriet, is listed in this census as age ten, try going back one more decade to the 1851 census — the year Harriet was supposedly born. Here the standard searches come up empty, so the next step is to eliminate the last name entirely and search for *edward born 1830 +/– 2 years in cambridge*. Even this turns up nothing, so next try eliminating the birth county as well. A search for first name *edward*, born *1830 +/–1 year* and spouse name *sarah* eventually turns up the family. It's no wonder they couldn't be found through traditional search methods. Edward Rowling born about 1830 in Bassingbourn, Cambridgeshire, was actually indexed in the 1851 U.K. census at Ancestry.com as Edward Bowlings born in Roystone, Cambodia. Royston is actually a township located within the parish of Bassingbourn so the indexer wasn't as far off as he appears, but he or she should have been able to recognize Cambr as an abbreviation for Cambridge, not Cambodia, when viewing the England census. The last name as handwritten on the census page does, however, appear more like Bowling than Rowling, with the final "s" added by the indexer actually a checkmark that follows each name on the page. The point here is that names are easily and often misindexed, so creative searching should be something you are always prepared to do when searching an online index. If you can't find someone by name, try other combinations of known facts. Be persistent! You can also try searching for another family member when the one you're looking for doesn't turn up. A search for first name *sarah* (no last name) born *1831+/–1* year in *southampton* would have also turned up the family.

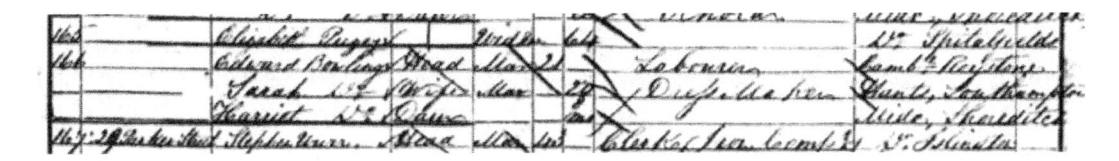

Now that you've traced William's parents back to their first census as a family, return to the 1871 census. Remember Edward listed as married, but with no wife Sarah? Was it a mistake that he wasn't listed as a widower? Or is Sarah enumerated somewhere else? Now that you have her name, a search for *sarah rowling* born in *southampton* turns up Sarah Marie Rowling as a patient in St. Bartholomews Hospital, London. Something else to investigate for the family tree!

Now that you know Sarah is still living in 1871, do you think she and Edward could still be living by the time of the 1881 census?

Edward is the one who's done a disappearing act in 1881, but Sarah Rowling, age fifty, born Southampton, is listed as a mother-in-law in the household of Frank Bennett in Medlock, Lancashire, England. You know this is likely the correct Sarah Rowling because Henry Rowling, listed as a brother-in-law, is the right age and was born in the right place to be the son Henry Rowling you found living with Edward Rowling in 1871 (also further confirmed when Edward Rowling is found living with the Bennetts in 1901 — see below). Since they are listed as in-laws, however, Frank's wife, Sarah, is probably a Rowling child as well. If so, where was she in the 1871 census? Something else for us to follow up in other records.

Further searches find Edward and Sarah appearing together again in the 1891 U.K. census, living in Hulme, Lancashire, England. The

1901 U.K. census finds Edward back with the Bennett family, unfortunately listed as a widower. You've now managed to locate the family (at least most of the members) in every U.K. census from 1851 to 1901 — something to be proud of. The family wasn't overly difficult to trace, but does exemplify many of the stumbling blocks you're likely to encounter during your own research — families that move around, families that aren't always enumerated together, names and locations that are misindexed, etc.

CHAPTER 7: Hunt Down Family Connections

Marriage records are something a genealogist always hopes to find because they help to "tie the knot" between two branches of the family tree. They can offer evidence that a couple was legally married, and may also indicate the bride's maiden name. Sometimes you'll even learn the bride and groom's date of birth or the names of the parents or other family members. Marriages also tend to generate a variety of documents, which increases your chances of finding a record that has survived through the years.

Marriage and Divorce Records

The most common civil record of marriage is the marriage license, issued to the bride and groom by the appropriate civil authority upon application for their marriage. Following the wedding ceremony, the license was returned by the minister or officiant with the date and location of marriage to the county courthouse or town hall to be recorded in the register. At the same time, an official certificate of marriage may have been issued to the couple; this certificate may be found among your family's papers. In some states, particularly the southern states, you may also encounter a precursor to the marriage license known as a marriage bond. This financial guarantee was made prior to the marriage by the prospective bridegroom (or a relative or friend of the groom or bride) to affirm that there was no moral or legal reason that the couple could not be married. In cases where the bride or groom was under the minimum legal age for marriage, you'll sometimes find a record known as the consent affidavit, a letter or form completed and signed by the parent or guardian giving permission for the underage individual to be married.

ESSENTIALS

Where to Write for Vital Records *(www.cdc.gov/nchs/howto/w2w /w2welcom.htm)* from the National Center for Health Statistics is a good starting place to learn about the availability of marriage and divorce records (as well as birth and death records) for the state you're researching. Vitalrec.com *(www.vitalrec.com)* also includes contact information and information on record availability for U.S. counties and parishes.

Civil marriage records in the United States are primarily found in the office of the county or town clerk. In some cases, however, older marriage records may have been transferred to the state archive, historical society, or library, while recent marriage records may only be available from the state vital records office. Individual state laws determine which agency is responsible. To further complicate matters, the date from which each state began to keep marriage records varies. Many states and territories were documenting marriages by 1880, but some did not officially record marriages statewide until well after 1900. In most cases, marriages were recorded at the town or county level prior to state registration, so you'll want to check county records as well. There is no nationwide index to marriage or other vital records in the United States.

In the absence of a marriage license or certificate, evidence of a marriage may be found in other documents. If your ancestor was married in a church or other house of worship, the marriage was likely recorded in the parish register or church book, along with preliminaries such as the posting of marriage banns. Newspapers can also be a good source for marriage information, including engagements, announcements, photos, and even descriptions of the ceremony and reception. Look for a special section of the newspaper dedicated to wedding announcements, or in the local news or society pages. A marriage date may also have been recorded in the family bible, on the back of a wedding photo, on a printed wedding or anniversary announcement, or in a letter, journal, or diary.

As with marriage records, divorce decrees relate to the family as a unit, and can often provide several details of genealogical value. These might include the wife's maiden name, the date and place of marriage, the dates of birth (or ages) of both parties to the divorce, the names and ages of any children, and the grounds for divorce. Divorce records are far less numerous than marriage records, however, and the manner in which divorces have been granted throughout history makes the records more difficult to locate as well.

Until the middle of the nineteenth century, divorce was rarely granted by the civil court. Instead, an act of the state legislature was necessary in most states, and it is among the records of these legislative acts where you'll find many early divorce proceedings. By the mid-1800s almost every state had enacted some type of divorce law, allowing for the "judicial" granting of a divorce. Most of these divorce decrees were issued in a court at the county level. The particular court varies by location and time period, so divorce decrees may be found among the records of the Superior Court, Circuit Court, Family Court, Chancery Court, District Court, or even the Office of the Prothonotary. Do a search online for *divorce records* in your state and county of interest to learn which court would have handled the process for the time period in which the divorce likely occurred. Most states also now require that a copy of the divorce certificate be filed with the state department that oversees vital records — a good alternative for divorces that have occurred since about the mid-twentieth century. References to a divorce may also be found in newspaper notices or among family papers.

E-LINK

Several Web sites make it their mission to link to as many online marriage indexes and databases as possible. GenWed *(www.genwed.com)* links to numerous free marriage records and indexes at both the state and county level. Follow the state links in the right-hand column. Online Birth and Marriage Records Indexes *(http://home.att.net/~wee-monster/vitalrecords.html)* and Cyndi's List — Marriages *(www.cyndislist.com/marriage.htm)* also link to larger online marriage record collections, organized by state.

Most marriage and divorce records online are available only in the form of indexes or abstracts. These typically include the name of the bride, the name of the groom, and the date of the marriage or divorce. Unless the site also offers digital images of the actual marriage record (and most don't), you should follow up by ordering or accessing the original record, as it will usually include additional details as well as offer additional verification of what you found online.

Birth and Baptismal Records

Because of privacy laws, birth records are generally the most difficult vital records to obtain and often cannot be found online for individuals born during or after the twentieth century. In fact, as with death records, official birth records were not even kept in many states until that time. For these more recent birth records it is usually best to start with your living family members. Because a birth certificate is often required as proof of identity, many people have a copy of their birth certificate among their papers.

Just because fewer birth records are available online than other vital records doesn't mean that you should discount finding them. Missouri, for example, offers a database of pre-1910 births (*www.sos.mo.gov/archives/resources/birthdeath*). Arizona offers not only an index but also images of the actual birth certificates (*http://genealogy.az.gov*) for births that occurred at least seventy-five years ago (so are no longer subject to privacy restrictions). West Virginia (*www.wvculture.org/vrr*) also has online images of birth records for selected counties and years. Family Tree Legends has an online index of Texas births from 1926 to 1995 (*www.familytreelegends.com/records/txbirths*). Ancestry.com offers a variety of online birth indexes among its subscription databases, including the North Carolina Birth Index (1800–2000), Kentucky Birth Collection (1852–1999), Minnesota Birth Index (1935–2002), and others. Check the Web site for the state archives, library, and/or historical society in your state of interest to see if they have put any birth records online. USGenWeb state and county sites will often include links to online birth indexes as well. Or try a search such as *birth records arizona* to see what else might be available.

QUESTIONS?

Can I record the date of baptism in lieu of a birth date?

A baptism may have taken place days or years after the actual birth. For this reason it is important to record the date as a baptismal date, not a birth date. Most genealogy software programs include a special field for entering baptism or christening dates. In the birth field, just record the birth date as occurring before the date of baptism since that is all you truly know for sure, as in "bef. 13 April 1769."

Older baptism and christening records are becoming increasingly easy to find online for countries such as England, Scotland, and France. In the United States, however, church records are much more scattered and few baptisms and christenings have been transcribed and placed online. See Chapter 8 for more on researching in church records.

Unearth Wills and Estate Records

After you've learned the details of your ancestor's birth, marriage, and death, you'll want to check to see if he left behind any estate records when he died. While "estate" seems to imply a large amount of property, estates are actually the sum total of an individual's possessions, including both property and debts, left behind at the time of death. The amount of real or personal property required to necessitate a court proceeding is determined by state or local laws in effect at the time of death. Not everyone will have owned enough property to generate estate records, but your ancestor also didn't necessarily need to be well-off to have had his estate processed through the court system. If he had outstanding debts, property that needed to be divided, or anything else that needed to be settled after his death, it's likely that some record of that still exists.

E-LINK

> For hands-on experience with estate records, the "Analyze an 1804 Inventory" case study at History Matters *(http://historymatters.gmu.edu/mse/sia/inventory.htm)* presents a typical estate with a discussion of how a simple list of an individual's possessions can reveal routines, social status, and values. Michael John Neill's excellent case study, "Fishing for Clues in John Lake's Estate" *(www.rootdig.com/adn/john_lake.html)*, explains — with accompanying document images — how estate records can provide numerous insights into a family's life.

Estate records document the processing and disbursement of an estate, whether the individual died *testate* (with a will) or *intestate* (without a will). If your ancestor left a will, it would normally be presented to the court by an heir, creditor, or other interested party after his death. The court would hold proceedings and hear testimony to verify the validity of the will in a process known as probate. The court also officially appointed an executor — generally an individual or individuals named in the will by the testator — to handle the affairs of the estate. Often, executors were relatives or friends, but the executor or executrix could be anyone the testator considered trustworthy enough to handle his estate. Once the court approved the probate, the will was then recorded (transcribed) into a Will Book by the court clerk. The original will also generally remained with the court, along with any other papers generated during the process of settling the estate, in a file often referred to as a probate packet.

When an individual dies without a will (which happens more frequently than you might think), the court generally appoints an administrator to handle the estate, and distribution of the property is made according to local law. These intestate proceedings, often called administrations, generate similar paperwork to the probate packets discussed previously, although they are often referred to as administration packets.

What exactly can estate records tell you beyond the fact that your ancestor died? The documents found in an estate, administration, or probate packet might include a complete inventory of the property of the deceased, a list of debts and creditors, appraisals, receipts, newspaper notices calling for legal heirs to come forward, witness testimony, letters from attorneys representing heirs, a copy of the will (if one exists), and other miscellaneous papers related to the settlement of the estate. Each of these pieces of paper represents the potential for learning more about your ancestor — especially the names of relatives (including the married names of daughters) and where they were each living. The list of personal property can be especially interesting, filled with items such as crockery, feather beds, pigs, brooms, and the like.

ALERT!

Most states allowed the female widow a share (usually one-third) of her husband's estate for her lifetime, known as her dower rights. When a mortgage or other debts existed, dower rights may have held up final settlement of the estate until after the widow's death. When no estate record is found, a search of land records may turn up the division of land necessary to give the widow her "dower third."

Estate records can usually be found with the court records of the county where the deceased was last living. Early records may have been moved to other repositories, such as the state archives. Check with the county clerk or the local genealogical or historical society to learn where the estate records are maintained. Some wills, especially those prior to about 1850 or so, have been published online, either in image or transcription form. Try a search such as *massachusetts wills online* and you'll turn up sites such as Wills of Our Essex County Ancestors (*www.essexcountyma.net/Wills*). Other examples of online wills and estate records include Probate Database Search (*http://archives.delaware.gov/collections/probate.shtml*), an online searchable index to Delaware probate records from c. 1680 to c. 1925; the St. Louis Probate Court Digitization Project, 1802–1900 (*www.sos.mo.gov/archives/stlprobate/Default.asp*), a collaborative project of the Missouri State Archives and the St. Louis Probate Court; and the North Carolina State Archives (*www.ah.dcr.state.nc.us/Archives*), which includes digital images of wills dated between 1663 and 1790 in its MARS database as well as an index to estate records for some North Carolina counties.

As with other record types, check the local USGenWeb site and spend some time thoroughly searching in your favorite search engine to learn what may be available online for your area of research.

Chase Down Court Records

Most of the records previously discussed in this chapter, as well as land records (covered in Chapter 8) and naturalization records (see Chapter 10), can be found in the town hall or county courthouse where your ancestors lived. This is because the local courthouse is generally where official business was conducted — where your ancestor would have gone to apply for a marriage license, file settlement papers for an estate, record a land deed, pay his taxes, register to vote, or transact other business of day-to-day life.

In addition to the records mentioned above and discussed elsewhere in this book, court records also document cases involving civil and criminal actions. Don't be afraid to search these records because you're afraid of what you might find. It's not unusual to discover relatives sprinkled throughout court records for minor civil proceedings involving property line disputes, bastardy bonds, and unpaid debts.

Your ancestor did not even have to be accused of anything to appear in court records. He may have provided witness testimony for a friend or neighbor or posted bond money for a relative. Or he might be named in county businesses transactions — assigned as a local tax collector, or to oversee repair of a county road. Most of you will find few surprises, but even one or two unexpected mentions of your ancestor may help you in your search. If nothing else, court records can sometimes offer amusing fodder for your family history.

In the United States, every state has a system of local courts that handles most of the local business and transactions likely to have involved your ancestors. Use the Internet (e.g., *edgecombe county nc courthouse* or *south dakota courts*) to search for information on the court system and courts in the town or county where your ancestor lived. The USGenWeb site is also a good starting point for learning about local courthouses and the location of their records. Consider also that your ancestor may have transacted at least some of his business in the courthouse that was most convenient to him, not necessarily the one that served the area in which he lived. Some business, such as the recording of land deeds, has to take place in the appropriate county or town, but other official business (e.g., obtaining a marriage license) can be handled at any county courthouse in some states. If you don't find court records in the most likely jurisdiction, expand your search to neighboring areas.

E-LINK

State and Local Government on the Net (*www.statelocalgov.net*) can be useful in locating official government Web sites, including those for the local court system. In addition, many states offer online directories of their county courts, such as the one found at Texas Courts Online (*www.courts.state.tx.us*). Most USGenWeb (*www.usgenweb.org*) county sites also provide contact information for the county courthouse.

The majority of court records will not be found online, but many court offices maintain some sort of virtual presence. The courthouse Web site may include information on the various offices within the courthouse and the records under their jurisdiction, the hours of operation, and, in some cases, details on how to request record lookups by mail or e-mail. Some courthouse offices, especially the Recorder of Deeds, may have indexes or other historical records online. The local library, historical society, or USGenWeb site may have published online guides or indexes to local court files. You can also check the Family History Library Catalog online to see if any court records have been microfilmed for your locality of interest, and request these for perusal through your local Family History Center.

Identify Adoptions and Orphans

Sometimes your own family history or the search for one of your ancestors is stalled because the circumstances of an ancestor's birth are shrouded in mystery. The first step in such a situation is the obvious one — to discover the names of the unknown birth parent or birth parents. If you believe the individual was formally adopted, the next step is to contact the agency or state that handled the adoption for a copy of the adoption order (in most states this information is sealed), or "nonidentifying information," which, governed by state law and agency policy, may include important details that aren't considered revealing enough to identify the birth parents. This nonidentifying information may include information on the adoptee, such as the date of birth and place of birth, and the birth parents, including a medical history, education level, religious affiliation, age at the birth, financial status, other siblings, and a physical description. Laws governing the release of identifying and nonidentifying information about adoptions vary from state to state, and country to country. Adoption.com offers a useful online guide to state adoption laws (*http://laws.adoption.com/statutes/state-adoption-laws.html*), including what information is available and where and how to access it.

E *ESSENTIALS*

Because of the difficulty of adoption research, and the possible emotional issues involved, it can often be beneficial to join an adoption search support group. The Adoptee Liberty Movement Association (ALMA) (*www.almasociety.org*) is an all-volunteer group offering assistance, advice, and moral support to individuals searching for adoptive roots. The Adoption Triad (*www.adoptiontriad.org*) offers all members of the adoption triad — adoptee, birth family, and adoptive family — support through chatrooms, forums, and outreach.

The Internet is also especially helpful in adoption searches because of the access it provides to reunion registries that match up searching family members who have been separated by adoption, foster care, or other means. The International Soundex Reunion Registry (*www.isrr.net*) is the largest such mutual-consent registry. You can find links to others in the Registries section (*http://adoption.about.com/od/registries*) of the About.com Adoption site.

If you manage to locate the name of a birth parent, or at least enough family facts to offer the chance of being able to identify them, a variety of genealogy resources can be helpful in your search. Census records, newspaper notices and obituaries, online telephone directories, public record databases, the Social Security Death Index, and other resources discussed throughout this book can be used.

Adoption is not the only thing that separates a child from his parents. It's not unusual to find a child sent to live with family members, or even neighbors, after a remarriage or the death of a parent. A child may also have been bound out as an apprentice to learn a trade. Children didn't even necessarily have to lose their parents to be considered orphans, and placed for a time under the responsibility of the county or local government. There are many records of orphans, especially in large cities, with at least one living parent who for some reason wasn't able to support them. These children might be traced to a poorhouse or orphanage, or may have been reared by foster parents (related or unrelated) or even sent west on an orphan train.

A good place to search for information on orphans is the county courthouse. Many areas maintained an Orphans' Court that handled the sale and division of real estate arising from estates, as well as the guardianship of minor children. In areas without an Orphans' Court, these matters were usually handled by the Probate Court. A guardian was generally appointed by the court to take charge of a minor's property, not necessarily custody of the child; thus, a child could have a guardian even if one or both parents were alive. But many true orphans can be found in the records as well, as they needed to have a guardian appointed to manage their parents' estate for them until they became of age — generally age eighteen for females and age twenty-one for males. Orphans' Court proceedings may contain records of orphans being bound out as apprentices as well.

Sometimes you'll get lucky and an Internet search will turn up guardianship and orphans' court records online, as in the case of the Wills, Guardianship and Orphans' Court database (*www.atlanticlibrary.org/collections/digitized/wills/index.asp*) on the Web site of the Atlantic County, New Jersey, library. If not, check the FamilySearch Library Catalog online to see what guardianship and orphans' court records have been microfilmed for your area of interest, and search for the county courthouse online to learn how these records might be accessed directly.

Orphan asylums were established by governments, churches, and private charities and their records are understandably scattered. Check with the local library or historical society to see if they have information on orphanages that operated in the area, or do an Internet search such as *orphans western pennsylvania*. Cyndi's List (*www.cyndislist.com/orphans.htm*) is an excellent place to find links to online resources and records on orphans, orphanages, and orphan trains.

CHAPTER 8: Look Local

Pinpointing where your ancestors lived is crucial to locating the written records that detail their lives. It can show you which courthouse to check for civil records, where your ancestors worshipped, and even where they might be buried. Maps can help identify the ancestral homestead, visualize the places where your ancestors lived and died, and suggest possible migration routes once followed by your ancestors. Geography can even be used as a tool to distinguish between two individuals with the same name.

Maps and Geography

Are you familiar with the area where your grandparents were born? You may know that it is a small Pennsylvania town called Shanksville, but you may not know what county it's in, or even whether it's located closer to Pittsburgh or Philadelphia. That's why the first thing you should do when you begin research in a new area is pull out a map. Online map services such as Yahoo! Maps (*http://maps.yahoo.com*), Google Maps (*http://maps.google.com*), or Windows Live Local (*http://maps.live.com*) all offer a host of features including address lookup, driving directions, and zoom and pan. Most also offer satellite imagery.

E-LINK

When your research uncovers an unfamiliar place name, turn to a placenames database such as the U.S. Geographic Names Information System (GNIS) (*http://geonames.usgs.gov*), which details over 2,000,000 places and features (towns, streams, mountains, cemeteries, and other geographical features) in the United States, including the names of places that no longer exist. Outside of the United States, you'll find similar assistance from the GeoNET Name Server (*http://earth-info.nga.mil/gns/html*).

Locate a Lost Town, Village, or Creek

What if you can't locate your ancestor's town on a modern map? Place names change. Geographical and political boundaries shift. Communities fall into disuse and disappear. Look for the answer in a gazetteer created during the time period of the document where you found the place name referenced. A gazetteer is a book that names and describes places in a given area during a given time period. With your mystery town's description and location from the gazetteer, you may be able to unearth a map from the period and identify the town's geographical location.

A variety of gazetteers can be searched and viewed online. One good modern gazetteer is Falling Rain's Global Gazetteer (*www.fallingrain.com/world*), a database of nearly 3 million populated places around the world, organized by country. Clicking on a location name takes you to a page with the latitude and longitude, several small maps, and a list of nearby cities and towns.

Historical gazetteers can be used to locate towns that exist no longer. While most are tucked away in libraries and archival repositories, many historical gazetteers can also be accessed online. Sites such as Vision of Britain (*www.visionofbritain.org.uk*) include historical descriptions drawn from gazetteers. Try a search for *gazetteer [your county, state, or region]* to identify online gazetteers that may be useful in your research.

Explore the Lay of the Land — Virtually

Maps provide the opportunity to visually explore the places where your ancestors lived, when they lived there. A variety of maps can be of use to genealogists, including:

- **Historical Maps** — Historical maps come in many varieties. One of the most useful for genealogists is a historical landowner's map, which shows property parcels along with the name of each landowner. Historical maps may also show churches, cemeteries, and other areas of interest. Thousands of historical maps are available online, some for free viewing and others for purchase. One of the largest free collections is the Perry-Castaneda Library Map Collection at the University of Texas at Austin (*www.lib.utexas.edu/maps*).

- **Topographic Maps** — Topo maps, (short for topographic maps), are a favorite with many genealogists because of their high level of detail. These maps emphasize physical features on the surface of the earth, from mountains and streams to cemeteries and railroad lines. Large-scale topo maps are sometimes so detailed you can see individual buildings, churches, and all navigable roads.

- **Fire Insurance Maps** — Fire insurance companies often requisition detailed maps of heavily populated areas to aid them in determining the risk factors in underwriting a particular property. These maps can be useful for genealogists because they depict building outlines, property boundaries, and street names for over 12,000 American towns and cities. The Digital Sanborn Maps, 1867–1970 offers online access to a collection of over 660,000 such maps. This database is available through subscribing libraries and institutions, so check with your local or state library to see if they offer it.

ESSENTIALS

You must know who had jurisdiction over a location to find records, but political and geographic boundaries are constantly changing. To help ensure that you're looking in the right place, *AniMap* Plus for Windows, by Gold Bug Software *(www.goldbug.com/AniMap.html)*, can display over 2,300 color maps to show the changing county boundaries for each of the 48 contiguous states for every year since colonial times.

Land and Property Records

You've already learned in the previous section how to locate your ancestor's town on the map. Now, it's time to take a closer look at the property and community that he called home. Land is traditionally considered to be a valuable asset and, as such, great care has been taken in the recording of property ownership and transfer. People, understandably, want to have legal proof that their land belongs to them! For this reason, property records are among the most numerous records in existence, going back further in time and applying to more people than almost any other genealogical record.

Although they are overlooked by many beginners to family history research, land records are a favorite resource of most professionals for the valuable genealogical evidence they can provide. According to William Dollarhide in his article "Retracing the Trails of Your Ancestors Using Deed Records" (*Genealogy Bulletin*, Jan.–Feb. 1995), nine out of ten adult males in America before 1850 owned land, and even today the figure is over 50 percent. With those odds, all genealogists with American ancestors should be using land ownership records in their family history research. A land record can place an individual in a specific location and time that, in turn, can lead to further records or help distinguish between two individuals with the same name. Land records are also a good source for names and relationships of family members, such as when a group of heirs jointly sell a parcel of inherited land.

Land records include a variety of different document types, including patents, deeds, bounty land warrants, and homesteading grants. Depending on the type of record and the time period, these may be found at the national, state, county, or local level. To understand which records might tell you more about your family, you will need to become familiar with the types of land records created in your geographical area of interest during specific periods.

QUESTIONS?

How can I identify my ancestor's property on a map?

With a protractor, ruler, and graph paper you can draw a plot of your ancestor's property based on the physical description in the deed or grant, a process known as land platting. Try it for yourself with the step-by-step instructions in Platting the Land of Your Ancestors (*http://genealogy.about.com/cs/land/a/metes_bounds.htm*), or use a computer program such as DeedMapper (*www.directlinesoftware.com*) by Direct Line Software to draw the plat map for you.

Who Owned the Land First?

The history of land acquisition and ownership in America could fill up an entire book. But it is also important to understand at least a little about how land was acquired, distributed, and transferred between governments and individuals in the area where your ancestor lived so you'll know what land records might be available and where they can be found. Search online for specific information on land history and ownership in your area, with a search query such as *history land pennsylvania*.

States where land was originally controlled and distributed by the colonial or state government are known collectively as the state-land states. These include the thirteen original colonies, plus Hawaii, Kentucky, Maine, Tennessee, Texas, Vermont, and West Virginia. As you might expect, these lands were surveyed and distributed in a variety of different ways. In some cases the government controlled the allocation of land, and in others this control was granted to a private citizen or citizens, such as the Lords Proprietors in North Carolina and the town proprietors of the New England states.

The majority of the state-land states, from Pennsylvania and New Jersey southward, continued the British survey system of *metes and bounds* to legally describe a piece of land. This system used local features such as trees, fences, stumps, and creeks to describe the property's boundaries. The distances along or between these features were usually described in poles, rods, or perches — all interchangeable with a distance of sixteen and a half feet. In New England, this system was supplemented by the drawing up of town plats — most in a roughly rectangular shape. This town plat was granted by the government to a group of town proprietors who then oversaw the sale and distribution of lots within the town.

Land in the state-land states was generally first distributed by means of *patents* or *grants*. This patent/grant is the initial transfer of title from the government or proprietor to the patentee/grantee. It is the first title deed and the beginning of private ownership of the land.

ALERT!

Old land surveys are often hard to fit on a modern map because of magnetic declination, the difference between the true north (the axis around which the earth rotates) used for maps and magnetic north (the place the needle on a compass will point) used by land surveyors. Because the direction of magnetic north has changed over time, you'll need to adjust your survey plots to correct for this declination error. The National Geophysical Data Center (*www.ngdc.noaa.gov/geomag/declination.shtml*) offers handy online tools for just this purpose.

Following the Revolutionary War, the new federal government got into the act — surveying and distributing the land under its control, also known as the public domain. The land in thirty states, often referred to as the federal-land states or public-land states, was initially controlled and surveyed by the U.S. government before its transfer into private hands. These public-land states were Alabama, Alaska, Arizona, Arkansas, California, Colorado, Florida, Idaho, Illinois, Indiana, Iowa, Kansas, Louisiana, Michigan, Minnesota, Mississippi, Missouri, Montana, Nebraska, Nevada, New Mexico, North Dakota, Ohio, Oklahoma, Oregon, South Dakota, Utah, Washington, Wisconsin, and Wyoming.

To keep things orderly, the government developed a new system for surveying its land prior to its being made available for purchase or homesteading, called the *rectangular survey system* or *township-range system*. The land was initially laid out into orderly squares organized along a *meridian* (imaginary line running from the North to the South Pole) and *base line*, which runs east and west. Meridian regions are divided into tracts of about twenty-four square miles, and these tracts are then divided into sixteen townships of about sixteen square miles each. Each township is further subdivided into thirty-six one-mile square *sections*, each consisting of 640 acres, and these sections are further subdivided into smaller pieces such as halves and quarters called *aliquot parts*. Each piece of property in a public-land state is identified in this manner in relation to a particular base line and meridian line. More detailed explanation of the rectangular survey system can be found online by searching for *public land survey system*.

In some states you'll run across several different systems of original land survey. For an extensive overview of land divisions and surveys in the United States, read *Land and Property Research in the United States* by E. Wade Hone.

Land in the public-land states was first distributed into private hands in a number of ways. The most common of these include homestead grants, military bounty warrants, and cash purchases of land.

Dig for Deeds

Land deeds are the method by which land is transferred between individual owners, recording all land transfers following the original grant, warrant, or sale of the land by the government to the first individual land owner. These might include deeds of sale and gift, mortgage sales, estate settlements, and other land transfers. In addition to providing the location and description of your ancestor's land, a deed may also identify the names of neighbors or relatives; a relationship between the grantee and the grantor, if one exists; or a clue to the former location of the buyer (grantee) or next location of the seller (grantor).

When deeds are recorded, they are copied into deed books maintained by the county or other local jurisdiction. These can usually be found under the jurisdiction of the Registrar of Deeds at the county courthouse. In the New England states of Connecticut, Rhode Island, and Vermont, land deeds are kept by the town clerks. In Alaska, deeds are registered at the district level, and in Louisiana deed records are kept by the parish. Indexes to these deed books are also compiled. In most cases you'll find two separate indexes: one organized by grantor (seller), sometimes called a *direct index*, and one indexed by grantee (buyer), sometimes called an *indirect index*. The two indexes may be combined, with a separate column showing "to" or "from" to indicate the grantor and grantee.

ALERT!

Look at an original land patent and you may notice a familiar signature at the bottom — that of the U.S. president in office at the time the patent was issued. Before you get excited, check the date as well. Patents dated after March 2, 1833, were actually signed by designated officials on the president's behalf. If you're lucky enough to have a pre-1833 original land patent handed down in your family, however, you may truly have a presidential treasure.

Since you'll generally be working with deed records in the courthouse or at your Family History Center, it pays to be thorough to cut down on the necessity of repeat visits. Check both the grantor and grantee indexes for your ancestors, as you can learn a lot from both the purchases and the sales. Index entries that list multiple names are a special treat, as they may signify family members or a group of heirs. The designation *et al.* — Latin for "and others" — following the name of a grantor or grantee often indicates such a deed. Before you leave, take time to make a copy of the deed index for your surnames of interest in the appropriate time period. This way you can easily order additional deeds by mail if you find others you need as your research progresses.

Locate Land Records Online

If your ancestor bought land from the federal government, you can do a free search for his land patent at the Web site of the General

Land Office, U.S. Bureau of Land Management (*www.glorecords.blm.gov*). The database provides access to more than 2 million federal-land title records for the public-land states, issued between 1820 and 1908. These include images of both homestead and cash patents. You can also access images of serial patents (land title records issued between 1908 and the 1960s) and survey plats (dating back to 1810).

E

The Family History Library has microfilmed the deed indexes and deeds for many U.S. counties. You can request these microfilms for use at your local Family History Center. Do a Place Search for the county name in the online Family History Library Catalog (*www.familysearch.org/Eng/Library/FHLC/frameset_fhlc.asp*) to see what deeds they have microfilmed for your areas of interest.

Patents are the final proof of land ownership, but there is also a wealth of information to be found in the paperwork generated by the land application process. This includes not only those who actually obtained patents, but the many who never completed the requirements or who had their application rejected. These documents have been compiled into Land Entry Case Files, and are in the custody of the National Archives (*www.archives.gov/genealogy/land*). Some of these land files — especially the homestead applications — can contain significant genealogical information including the age or date of birth of the applicant, his marital status, name of the spouse, and size of the family. Land entry files can be ordered online from the National Archives (*www.archives.gov/research/order/orderonline.html*).

Since land in the state-land states was distributed by the colonial or state government, there is no nationwide database for these records. Instead, original land grant records can usually be found in the state archive or equivalent repository. They may also be found recorded in the county deed registers. Because of their historical value, many of these early land patents and grants are being digitized and placed online. Try a search such as *historical "land records,"* plus the name of the state or county in question to learn what is available online for your area of interest.

Bounty land was granted by the federal government and eight states in return for military service. Many bounty land warrants can be searched and viewed online. These records are discussed in detail in Chapter 9.

For every record you find on the Internet, there are dozens that can only be accessed offline in archives, libraries, and similar repositories. Books such as Courthouse Research for Family Historians by Christine Rose and articles such as "Ten Questions to Ask a Research Facility Before You Visit"
(*http://genealogy.about.com/od/libraries/a/questions.htm*)
will help you prepare for your trip before heading out the door.

Deeds transferring land titles between private citizens are maintained at the county or local level rather than the state level. Therefore, you won't find quite as many deed records online. Many counties do offer online access to recent deeds and other property information. Historical deeds, however, take time and money to digitize that many counties just can't afford. Exceptions, such as the New Hampshire County Registries of Deeds (*www.nhdeeds.com*) and Land Records in Maryland (*www.mdlandrec.net*), can be found, however. Do a search for *county state deeds* or check out the Web site of the Registrar of Deeds or Clerk of Court for the appropriate county and state to see what they may have online.

Historical Newspapers

Your family didn't necessarily have to be famous or wealthy to make the news — at least not after the introduction of the penny newspaper in 1833 made newspapers easily available to the masses. Important life events such as births, marriages, deaths, and funerals often appeared in the local newspaper, as did land transactions, court proceedings, school achievements, and other information on the everyday life of the area's inhabitants. Beyond the names and dates, newspapers frequently contain firsthand accounts of important events and issues, and reflect popular thinking and cultural attitudes of the time. Even the advertisements are enlightening, offering insight into local fashion, trends, and the cost of living.

Prior to the Internet, using historical newspapers to research family history was generally undertaken only by the most tenacious researchers. They just weren't easily available, often existing only on microfilm at the local or state library. Newspapers also don't typically come with an index, so newspaper research generally involves a lot of research and guesswork just to select the newspaper and issue(s) most likely to contain information of interest. Once the search has been narrowed to a particular newspaper and time period, newspaper research can still involve hours spent in front of a microfilm reader scrolling through page by page, skimming line after line.

ALERT!

Don't limit yourself to births, marriages, and obituaries when researching your family in old newspapers. Some of the best finds may come from the society and neighborhood columns, where you can get little snippets about visiting relatives, children joining the military or leaving for college, people suffering or recovering from a serious illness, and trips to visit friends and family in other towns.

Online access to historical newspapers has changed the scope of newspaper research, making it much more easily available to anyone interested in their family history. Many publishers and organizations have recently undertaken the digitization of historical newspapers in order to preserve and provide increased access to their rich history and commentary. The entire archive of the *New York Times* — dating back to its first issue in 1851 — is just one such example of the many historical newspapers that have been made available for viewing via the Internet. These treasures of digital history present a great source for gaining knowledge about your family and the time and place in which they lived.

In addition to increased access, the digitization of historical newspapers allows for easier research with tools such as zoom, pan, and full-text search. The full-text search does come with a caveat, however. Most digitization projects use optical character recognition (OCR) technology to automatically recognize text within the digitized newspaper images. This process is much quicker and more cost-effective than manual indexing (can you imagine the effort the latter would take?), but does lend itself to inaccuracies. This is especially true for older newspapers where the typeface was a bit more flowery and may be harder for a computer to accurately decipher. The search results may include extraneous "matches" on words that the OCR technology believes are optically similar enough that they could be your target word. As a result, searching in historical newspaper databases can require quite a bit of creativity and patience, but the rewards are often immeasurable.

ESSENTIALS

For every newspaper you can access online, there are hundreds more only available in libraries and other repositories around the world. Sites such as Chronicling America (*www.loc.gov/chroniclingamerica*) can tell you which newspapers were published, and when, for any place in the United States, as well as which repositories hold original or microfilm copies of the newspapers.

ProQuest Historical Newspapers

This collection of full-text and full-image articles from prestigious U.S. newspapers was first created in 2001 with the digitization of the *New York Times*. Other major newspapers now included in the fully searchable database include the *Chicago Tribune, Washington Post, Los Angeles Times, Atlanta Constitution, Boston Globe, Hartford Courant, New York Tribune, New York Amsterdam News, Pittsburgh Courier, Wall Street Journal,* and *Christian Science Monitor*. Every issue of each title includes the complete newspaper in downloadable PDF format and full-text search with a variety of advanced search options. This collection is only available through subscribing libraries and institutions, and is not available for individual subscriptions. Check with your local, college, or state library to see if they subscribe to any or all of the newspapers in this collection. Many offer free in-library and remote access to their patrons.

NewspaperARCHIVE

This subscription-based service is one of the largest historical newspaper collections available online. The NewspaperARCHIVE database (*www.newspaperarchive.com*) contains more than 60 million full-page images from historical newspapers from around the world, ranging from the 1700s to the present. Coverage varies by newspaper, so use the Browse Available Papers feature to see which publications and dates are available before subscribing to a full-access membership. Online cancellation is available, but refunds are not offered for unused time. Selected papers from the NewspaperARCHIVE collection are available as part of a World Vital Records (*www.worldvitalrecords.com*) subscription.

Ancestry.com Historical Newspapers

Historical newspapers are available as part of the Ancestry.com subscription Web site. The Historical Newspaper Collection (*www.ancestry.com/search/rectype/periodicals/news*) offers access to selected years from thousands of newspapers across the United States, United Kingdom, Canada, and Australia, dating back to the 1700s. Individual subscriptions to just the newspaper portion are not available; you have to subscribe to the entire Ancestry.com U.S. or World Record Collection.

GenealogyBank

A product of the information provider NewsBank, GenealogyBank (*www.genealogybank.com*) offers more than 78 million articles, obituaries, marriage notices, and birth announcements published in over 1,300 historical U.S. newspapers, from 1690 through 1977. You can search the site for free and see brief excerpts that contain your search results, but you'll need to subscribe to view the entire article. A similar service, operating under the name *America's GenealogyBank,* is offered as a subscription service to libraries, so check to see if you have free access through your local or state library before subscribing.

Chronicling America: Historical American Newspapers

A joint project of the National Endowment for the Humanities (NEH) and the Library of Congress (LC), the National Digital Newspaper Program is a twenty-year plan to create a national digital resource of historically significant newspapers from all states and U.S. territories. The project's Web site, Chronicling America (*www.loc.gov/chroniclingamerica*), allows you to find information about American newspapers published between 1690 and the present, including the libraries that carry each title. The free database also allows you to search and read the currently digitized newspaper pages. The first phase went live in 2007 and includes newspapers published in California, District of Columbia, Florida,

Kentucky, New York, Utah, and Virginia during the decade of 1900 to 1910. As long as funding allows, the project will continue to expand its coverage.

SmallTownPapers

Newspaper archive company SmallTownPapers (*www.smalltownpapers.com*) provides free access to more than 300 small-market newspapers from across the United States dating back as far as 1865. This collection is also available as part of WorldVitalRecords.com.

Newspaper Abstracts

Volunteers have transcribed and placed online more than 50,000 pages of abstracts and extracts from historical newspapers at Newspaper Abstracts (*www.newspaperabstracts.com*). These are partial transcriptions, not fulltext articles or digital images, but the site is entirely free.

Libraries and Societies

A stop at the public library of the community where your ancestor lived is a must for any family historian. Libraries are a gateway to rich primary source materials on the history and culture of the region they serve, as well as the people who lived in the area. The library is usually the local repository for archived newspapers, city directories, school yearbooks, and other resources specific to the community. Many larger libraries also maintain a local history section, with family histories, community and local history books, photographs, and records such as census enumerations, cemetery transcriptions, and marriage indexes.

E-LINK

Use the Internet as a tool to find libraries that serve the locations where your ancestors lived, or that host records or special collections that match your research interests. PublicLibraries.com (*www.publiclibraries.com*) maintains listings and links to U.S. state libraries and college and university libraries, organized by state. LibWeb (*http://lists.webjunction.org/libweb*) includes links to over 7,500 Web pages from libraries in over 135 countries, including public, academic, and religious libraries.

Online, a library visit means an excursion to the library's Web site. Many libraries offer unique online content in the form of digitized original records, or transcribed indexes or databases. The University of Pittsburgh library (*http://digital.library.pitt.edu*), for example, provides access to historical maps and photos, transcribed census records, and the full text of over 500 published works that relate to local Pittsburgh and Pennsylvania history. Another unique resource can be found on the Web site of the New York Public Library, where over 600 Yiskor books (Holocaust memorial books) from the library's collection are available online in digitized format. Even smaller libraries may offer cemetery transcriptions or an index to obituaries that have appeared in their local paper. The Cleveland Public Library (*www.cpl.org*), which hosts an online Necrology File of cemetery records and newspaper death notices, is one such example. Collaborative databases, in which several libraries or societies pool their records and resources, are also becoming common online. In Indiana, the Vital Information Exchange (VINE) (*http://digital.statelib.lib.in.us/db/vine/vine_home.asp*) is a statewide database of vital records, obituaries, newspapers, yearbooks, and other local history resources from Indiana libraries, historical societies, genealogy societies, and related organizations. A group of libraries in central and northeastern Ohio have banded together to create the regional MOLO Obituary Index (*www.ohiofamilysearch.org*).

Even libraries that don't have online records can be helpful in your research. Most library Web sites make at least a portion of their catalog available for searching online. Look for a link from the site's home page. You may also find information on submitting lookup or research requests. Many librarians are willing to do brief lookups in indexed books, databases, and clipping files, or provide a copy of an obituary if you can provide a name and date. In some cases this service may cost you a few dollars to cover expenses and postage, but it is well worth it.

University and college libraries are sometimes overlooked by genealogists, but they often hold unique historical resources. They can have many unpublished genealogies and histories in their manuscript division, as well as the records of churches and businesses.

One tool used by many genealogists to locate library resources is World Cat, a catalog of materials held in more than 7,600 libraries in the United States and around the world, including public, academic, and state libraries; archives; and historical societies. This includes special collections devoted to local history, which means you may find citations for historical newspapers, oral histories, family histories, cemetery records, historical photographs, family bibles, town or county histories, and a wide variety of other materials. In 2006, WorldCat also opened a free Internet search portal to the public (*www.worldcat.org*). You can search it directly, and also access it through "find in a library" links for book results on sites such as Google Books and Amazon.

Churches and Schools

In just about every town, you can find a church and a school. Throughout much of history these buildings have served as the center of the community, a focus of daily life for area residents. For this reason, church and school records often provide intriguing insights into the lives and personalities of earlier generations. They may also supply concrete facts, such as dates of birth or baptism, marriage, and death, or proof of family relationships.

Religious Records

Church and synagogue records are a very valuable source for pre-1900 baptisms, marriages, and burials, but be prepared to face a few challenges. The existence of more than a hundred different religious denominations can make it difficult to determine the church with which your ancestor had an affiliation. Churches themselves have appeared, disappeared, and merged over time. Record keeping varies widely. Some records are in the custody of individual churches, others in diocesan collections, and still others in national archives or other repositories. Generally, there are few catalogs or indexes to these church records, and the vast majority cannot be accessed online. In most cases you'll find it necessary to visit the church or archives in person, or to hire a researcher.

ALERT!

The interlibrary loan (ILL) service at your local library can be a gold mine for genealogists interested in materials held by libraries far from their home. While few libraries will lend noncirculating genealogical materials, you can often use an ILL request to borrow copies of microfilmed records, or to ask that they make copies of the index for your ancestors' surnames or a few relevant pages from a book or newspaper.

To locate church records, you must first identify the denomination of your ancestor, and the actual church that she attended. Don't just assume that your ancestors practiced the same religion that you do today. It's very common to find individuals or families who have changed denominations. In rural areas, the choice of churches was generally limited, and residents may have attended the church or parish most convenient for them. Once you determine the religion, a directory may be able to help you pin down the closest church to where your ancestor lived.

When you have located the church, you next need to find out where the records are kept. Begin with an online phone directory or Internet search to see if the church still exists, and then contact them to learn about the availability of records for your time period of interest. If the church is no longer in existence, an e-mail or call to the local historical society or library, or to the regional headquarters for that denomination, may provide you with information. Many older church records have been published in book form or in local genealogical and historical periodicals. Look under your locality of interest in online library catalogs and in PERSI. The *National Union Catalog of Manuscript Collections* can be useful in locating church records held by libraries and historical societies (see Chapter 8).

One of the largest sources of transcribed and/or indexed church records online is the International Genealogical Index at FamilySearch (*www.familysearch.org*), which includes millions of extracted church records, primarily baptisms and marriages, from around the world. The USGen-Web Church Records Project (*www.rootsweb.com/~usgenweb/churches*) hosts transcribed membership lists, church bulletins, church minutes, and records of baptisms, marriages, and burials submitted by volunteers. Most of the transcribed records are from the 1700s and early 1800s. Subscription genealogy sites such as Family Tree Connection (*www.familytreeconnection.com*) and Ancestry.com include databases such as church member lists, registers, and histories. An online search such as *church records oakdale pennsylvania* may turn up online databases, church histories, or other resources for church records in your locality of interest.

E *ESSENTIALS*

The *Yearbook of American and Canadian Churches*, published annually by the National Council of Churches in the USA and available from their Web site, lists all major denominations with contact information and a capsule history. An online Web directory (*www.electronicchurch.org*) includes links to the denomination Web sites.

Even in the many cases where the actual church records are not online, you can do a lot of the background research on the Internet. The Family History Library has microfilmed records for many denominations that you can learn about by doing a place search in the online Family History Library Catalog. The Web sites for regional and national headquarters for many denominations offer information on the availability of records for family history research, as well as online directories of churches, parishes, or synagogues.

School Records

From the seventeenth century to the present day, schools and other educational institutions have created records that may have information about your ancestors, including registration records, class lists, alumni lists, transcripts, report cards, school censuses, and class photos. If your ancestor went to college you may be especially lucky, as colleges and universities tend to create, maintain, and preserve more comprehensive records than most primary and secondary schools. School fraternities and sororities also provide a potential source for records on such ancestors.

The one-room rural schoolhouse was a vital part of early American life, but these records, even if they have survived, may be hard to find. As the schools were closed, records may have been deposited with county or state repositories. Sometimes the local library or historical society may have these records, or know where they are kept. Twentieth-century school records are usually much more comprehensive, and can often be found by contacting the school or school district directly. Try your favorite search engine to find schools in a particular location, using a search such as *schools lexington county south carolina*. The Board of Education in the state in which your ancestor attended school may also be of assistance in locating records. You'll often find, however, that many schools restrict access to personal information on people who may still be living. You may be able to get around these privacy issues by proving that you're a relative of the individual of interest, and that she is deceased.

As with church records, most school records cannot be accessed online. The previously mentioned subscription site Family Tree Connection (www.familytreeconnection.com) includes a number of transcribed school records and yearbooks. Check the USGenWeb site for your county, as many have transcribed school records included among their online offerings. For university and college records, search their online library catalog to see what may be available in the school archives. Some collections of school records hidden away in libraries and archives may be found by searching the *National Union Catalog of Manuscript Collections*.

Yearbooks, school newspapers, and alumni registers and directories provide alternative avenues for research when the school records them-selves are unavailable. If the school still exists — especially in the case of colleges, universities, or private schools — these resources may be available through the school library or alumni association.

Local History

So much of what your ancestors did during their lives — their choice of occupation, who they married, and how they lived — has to do with the place they called home. A young man in a small, rural farming community, for example, was probably a bit limited when it came to his choice of brides. A large family living in the "big" city was more likely to rent than own their home. Researching the local history of the town, village, or city where your ancestors lived is a big step toward understanding what their life was like — the people, places, and events that impacted the course of their own personal history. This is what will help you place the raw facts of your genealogy — names, dates, and places — into historical context, and really bring your family tree to life.

E-LINK

The more you delve into your family's history, the more you're going to want to know about the history of your country and the events in which your ancestors participated. Digital History *(www.digitalhistory.uh.edu)* helps users reconstruct the past through a variety of primary sources, as does American Memory *(http://memory.loc.gov)* from the Library of Congress. The History sites at About.com *(www.about.com/education)* offer a wealth of historical information from medieval times to the twentieth century.

Much of your research into local history can and should be done in conjunction with the rest of your genealogy research. As you search an old newspaper for an obituary notice, for example, take time to look at the news headlines, the gossip columns, and even the advertisements to get a glimpse of what people were interested in during that time. When you're visiting the Web site of the local historical society or county government for information on available records, take a few extra minutes to click through on the History or About Us links, if available, to learn more about the area. As you enter information from census enumerations or marriage records in your genealogy software, be sure to add not just names and dates, but also facts for things such as residence (with the street name when given) and occupation. It can be very interesting to track these over time.

One of the tools many genealogists use to visualize their ancestors' place in history is the timeline. Many genealogy software programs can help you create a basic timeline, or you can use special timeline software (search the Web for *timeline software* or *timeline creator*). On this timeline you'll add important dates from your ancestors' lives, along with historic events such as wars, natural disasters, epidemics, etc. Look for local events of importance, as well as national and world events to add to your timeline. Knowing that your ancestors lived in the mid-1800s and actually "seeing" the events they lived through are two different things.

If your ancestors lived in a particular area for a long time, you'll probably want to dig even further into their past. Local history books, old photographs and postcards, cookbooks, fashion timelines … all of these and more can be found online with a good Internet search. Your ancestor may not have left a diary, but you may be able to read one online from someone else living in the same general area during the same time period. Your box of old photos may not include a picture of your great-grandmother's house, but you can probably find photos online of her town and other homes in the community.

CHAPTER 9: Mine the Web for Military Records

More than 42 million Americans, representing almost every generation, have participated in some type of wartime service. Men as young as sixteen and as old as sixty may have joined local militia units, making it likely that you'll discover at least one ancestor or relative with a military past. Military records can also document people who never actually served, such as the millions of young men who registered for the World War I and World War II drafts but were never called up for duty.

Find Clues to Military Service

Begin your search for military records by talking with living relatives and reviewing the documents and other information you have already collected. The goal is to identify ancestors who may have participated in the military and, ultimately, to determine when and where the soldier served. Clues to an ancestor's military service may be found in the following:

- **Family stories** — If a relative says that your ancestor served in the military it is most likely true. Just keep in mind that memories get fuzzy with time, and the details may have been exaggerated or embellished a bit.

- **Photographs** — Search your family photograph collection for pictures of people in uniform. The type of photo and style of uniform can help determine the branch of the military and the war or time period in which your ancestor served. Patches, pins, insignia, and even belt buckles may help determine rank or unit.

- **Census records** — Occupational references may indicate military service. The conspicuous absence of a male relative during war-time may also offer a clue. The 1910 census indicates whether the person was a "survivor of the Union or Confederate Army or Navy." The 1930 census indicates military service in major wars through World War I.

- **Newspaper clippings** — People were proud of their hometown heroes, and brief mentions of local soldiers often made the community papers.

- **Journals and correspondence** — Writing letters or keeping a diary offered a distraction from the boredom of military camp life and the terror of battle. Such letters or journals may be found among your family's belongings, or in a library or archive.

- **Death records and obituaries** — A soldier's obituary or death record may mention military service and provide details such as branch or regiment.

- **Local histories** — Published town or county histories often include stories and photos of local military units.

- **Grave markers** — A flag, emblem, engraving, or marker on your ancestor's gravestone may indicate military service. Many countries also honor their veterans with special markers.

Once you have determined that an ancestor served in the military, there are a wide variety of records that may help to document his service. These include military service records, draft registrations, medals and ribbons, pension papers, discharge papers, pay vouchers, casualty lists, unit rosters, and bounty land warrants. From these records you can learn such details as date and place of birth, age at enlistment, occupation, and names of immediate family members. The path you take in your search will depend upon when and where your ancestor served, whether he was regular army or with a volunteer unit, and whether he was an officer or enlisted personnel.

Tombstone inscriptions and symbols are a good source for clues to military service. Acronyms and abbreviations may indicate the branch of military service, such as U.S. Air Force (USAF) or U.S. Navy (USN). Others may be a little less obvious, such as SS for Silver Star, GAR for Grand Army of the Republic, or UDC for United Daughters of the Confederacy. Search for *military acronyms or military tombstone symbols* for identification assistance.

Compiled Military Service Records

For military ancestors who served prior to World War I, the compiled military service records are a good place to start. These are basically just what they sound like — an abstract of the available military information on an individual compiled from a variety of service-related records. Compiled military service records were originally begun in 1894 in an effort to reconstruct records of the American army and navy that were destroyed by fires in 1800 and 1814. The project eventually grew to cover all soldiers serving in *volunteer* units in wars between 1775 and 1902, including not only individuals from the American Revolution and War of 1812, but also those who served in various Indian conflicts, the Mexican War, the Civil War, the Spanish American War, the Philippine Insurrection, and the Boxer Rebellion. A compiled military service record consists of a card with the soldier's name, rank, and unit, along with abstracted information taken from muster rolls, hospital records, pay vouchers, record books, orders, correspondence, and other records. This card is then placed in an envelope, or jacket. Sometimes original documents may also be included in the envelope. The compiled military service record will generally provide you with your ancestor's rank, unit, the state from which he served, the date enlisted, and the length of service. You may also find the age, residence, a physical description, and date of discharge or death.

QUESTIONS?

What if I don't know whether I have an ancestor who was in the military?

If you have an ancestor of the right age at the right time to have served in a military conflict, it doesn't hurt to spend some time searching in military records — especially given the easy search capabilities of online databases. Just be careful not to assume that the individual you've found is your ancestor, especially if you discovered his name in an index, without following up in additional records.

The National Archives in Washington, D.C., is the official repository for federal military service records of personnel who served in the

U.S. Army, Air Force, Navy, Marine Corps, or Coast Guard between the Revolutionary War and about 1912. This includes compiled military service records for Confederate army soldiers. Military service records, including compiled service records, can be ordered online (*www.archives.gov/veterans/military-service-records/pre-ww-1-records.html*), or by mail using NATF Form 86 (which you can download online). Online indexes to these compiled service records include:

- **Footnote** (*www.footnote.com*), in cooperation with the National Archives, offers subscription-based online access to the compiled military service records of soldiers who served in the American army during the Revolutionary War, as well as for Confederate Civil War soldiers.

- **Ancestry.com** (*www.ancestry.com/search/db.aspx?dbid=4281*) features an index to the compiled military service records for the volunteer soldiers who served during the War of 1812; it can be searched online by subscribers.

- The **Civil War Soldiers and Sailors System (CWSS)** (*www.itd.nps.gov/cwss*) offers a free index of more than 6 million Civil War Confederate and Union soldiers compiled from the General Index Cards of the compiled military service records at the National Archives. Click on Soldiers or Sailors on the right-hand side to search for a name.

The War Department did not compile military service records for those who served in the regular army. For information on the pre–World War I records available for researching enlisted army personnel, as well as those who served in the navy and marine corps, see "An Overview of Records at the National Archives Relating to Military Service" (*www.archives.gov/veterans/research/prologue-military-records-overview.html*).

Pensions and Bounty Land Warrants

The men and women who serve in the military are often compensated in some extra way for their service. In the case of the Revolutionary War, War of 1812, early Indian wars, the Mexican War, and the Civil War, the records of these veterans' benefits — pensions and bounty land warrant applications — are perhaps the most valuable resources available for genealogical researchers.

Military pensions were granted by the federal government or state government to disabled and needy veterans, to the widows or dependent orphans of veterans, or to veterans who served for a certain length of time and lived long enough to receive the pension benefits. Pension files are often rich in genealogical information, containing such facts as birth date and place, marriages, residence at time of application, property holdings, and names of minor children. Supporting documents, such as discharge papers, testimony from neighbors and fellow soldiers, marriage certificates, physician's reports, and family bible pages, can sometimes be found included with pension files.

The federal government, and some states, granted free land known as *bounty land* to veterans as an inducement or reward for service in the military. Bounty land warrants were issued from the colonial period until 1858, when the program was discontinued, to veterans of the Revolutionary War, War of 1812, and Mexican War. Bounty land was *not* available for Civil War soldiers. Veterans or their heirs could claim this free land by filing an application, known as a bounty land warrant application. If the application was approved, the individual was given a warrant that he could later exchange for land on which he could settle. The government set aside certain land districts in the frontier areas where veterans could redeem their warrant for bounty land. Many historians believe that this was designed to lure the battle-trained soldiers and their families into areas where they could serve as a buffer against Indian attacks. Most veterans were too smart to fall for that ploy, and instead chose to sell their land warrants to speculators. Therefore, your veteran ancestor may have applied for a bounty land warrant, but never received title to or settled on bounty land.

> **ESSENTIALS**
>
> If your direct ancestor wasn't involved in the military or you can't find any records for him, look for the records of brothers, uncles, cousins, and neighbors. These may contain information and testimony that refer to your direct lineage. This is a research technique known as cluster genealogy.

Many of the early Revolutionary War bounty land application files, from 1789 to 1800, were destroyed in a War Department fire. Most of the surviving applications relating to Revolutionary War and War of 1812 service have been combined with the pension files because they contain similar types of information.

An excellent online resource for these records is the Revolutionary War Pension and Bounty-Land Warrant Application Files database available on HeritageQuest Online. This database, which includes an index as well as digitized copies of the original handwritten records, was taken from NARA microfilm M805, which reproduces *selected* portions of the pension and bounty land applications filed by Revolutionary War veterans or their heirs between 1800 and 1906. This database is only available to subscribing libraries, not to individual subscribers. Check with your local or state library to see if they offer free online or in-library access for patrons.

If you find your ancestor in the HeritageQuest database, and the file appears fairly large, follow up in NARA microfilm publication M804, available online with both a name index and digitized images at Footnote. The HeritageQuest Online database is based on M805, which only includes about ten pages or fewer per file of the most genealogically significant documents. M804 at Footnote reproduces the entire pension file and may include additional information. Footnote and Ancestry.com both offer a searchable name index and images of the pension index cards of Union Civil War veterans reproduced from NARA microfilm T-288, with over 3 million index entries documenting the pension applications of soldiers, sailors, and their widows. A search engine query such as *genealogy pension* will turn up additional sources, such as the USGenWeb Archives Pension Project (*www.usgwarchives.org/pensions*).

Copies of military pension claim files for military service from the American Revolution up to just before World War I (1775 to 1912), and bounty land warrant applications for federal military service prior to 1856, can be ordered online from the National Archives (*www.archives.gov/veterans/military-service-records/pre-ww-1-records.html*), or by mail using NATF Form 85. These are for pensions and bounty land warrants based on federal (not state or Confederate) service. Pension records for Confederate soldiers are discussed in the Civil War section later in this chapter.

Discover Revolutionary and Civil War Ancestors

There's something a bit special and awe-inspiring about having an ancestor who served in the American Revolution or Civil War — knowing that someone from whom you descend participated in the struggle to win the freedoms we enjoy today. Whether you agree with their reasons for fighting or the side for which they fought, it can be a real source of pride to have ancestors who were willing to fight and die for a cause they so strongly believed in. Learning about these ancestors and their beliefs can also help connect you to a very important part of this nation's history in a way that almost nothing else can.

The American Revolution

Whether you're interested in joining a lineage society such as the Daughters of the American Revolution or Sons of the American Revolution, or just want to learn more about possible Revolutionary ancestors, a good place to start your online search is the Patriot Lookup service of the Daughters of the American Revolution (*www.dar.org*). Just fill out a brief online form with details on your ancestor, and the volunteers will check their index of Revolutionary Patriots, the men and women, who have been accepted by the DAR genealogical staff as having contributed to the cause of American independence between 1774 and 1783. If the DAR confirms your ancestor as a Revolutionary Patriot, you can also use their Web site to order a copy of the most recent DAR application or file for your patriot ancestor.

ALERT!

The U.S. Department of Veterans Affairs (VA) will furnish, upon request and at no charge to the applicant, a government headstone or marker for the grave of any eligible deceased veteran in any city around the world, including those buried in private cemeteries. Learn more about the eligibility requirements and how to apply for a military marker from the Department of Veterans Affairs *(www.cem.va.gov/cem/hm_hm.asp)*.

Next, check out Footnote (*www.footnote.com*), which provides subscription-based access to a variety of digitized Revolutionary-era records from the National Archives. These include the previously mentioned compiled service records and pension records, as well as Revolutionary War muster rolls and payrolls and the papers of the Continental Congress.

A few other excellent online databases for Revolutionary-era research include:

- **American Genealogical-Biographical Index** (*www.ancestry.com*) — includes indexes to numerous Revolutionary War — related publications. A subscription is required.

- **A Century of Lawmaking for a New Nation** (*http://memory.loc.gov/ammem/amlaw*) — This special collection in the free online American Memory exhibit of the Library of Congress includes some very interesting Revolutionary War pension petitions and other sources for information on Revolutionary-era individuals. Follow the links to American State Papers and the U.S. Serial Set.

Many Revolutionary War soldiers fought in the state militia, and their records will usually be found among the appropriate state's records, not in the National Archives. Various state archives, historical societies, and other organizations have posted some of their state Revolutionary War records online. Examples include Pennsylvania Revolutionary War Military Abstract Card File Indexes (*www.digitalarchives.state.pa.us*); South Carolina Revolutionary War Letters, Diaries and Orders (*www.southcarolinahistoricalsociety.org/archives/arch_revwar.htm*); and the Kentucky Secretary of State Revolutionary War Warrants index (*http://apps.sos.ky.gov/land/military/revwar*). Do a search in your favorite search engine for *"revolutionary war" + your state* to find available records and documents.

A discussion of American Revolution research wouldn't be complete without a reminder that there was another side to the war. You may have ancestors who were Loyalists, or Tories — colonists who remained loyal subjects of the British crown and actively worked to promote the interest of Great Britain during the American Revolution. After the war ended, many of these Loyalists were driven from their homes by local officials or neighbors, and almost all moved on to resettle in Canada, England, Jamaica, and other British-held regions. The Online Institute for Advanced Loyalist Studies (*www.royalprovincial.com*) provides an excellent starting point for further research into Loyalist ancestors.

The Civil War

The Civil War marked the most tragic chapter of American history. As with the Revolutionary War, the conflict tore apart families, friendships, and even towns. These divided loyalties mean that you may find you have ancestors that fought on both sides.

If your ancestor was born between about 1805 and 1847, chances are good that he may have fought in the Civil War. Even men in their sixties and boys in their early teens participated. But where did he serve, and for which side? The three most valuable pieces of information necessary for researching a Civil War ancestor are the soldier's name, whether he served for the Confederate or Union army, and the state from which the soldier served. With this information you can determine what types of records are available that might tell you about your ancestor and where he is located. Remember, there were two national governments in effect during those years — the federal government of the United States and the Confederate States of America. That combined with the massive destruction of property, especially in the South, means that many of the existing records have been left fragmented and scattered between the National Archives, state archives, lineage societies, and other repositories. Plenty of excellent Civil War records do exist; they are just not all in one place. Therefore, the biggest hurdle in Civil War research is often in knowing where to look.

The first step in documenting your ancestor's Civil War service is to search service records and rosters for his name. The previously mentioned Civil War Soldiers and Sailors System (*www.itd.nps.gov/cwss*) is the best place to start. Here you can learn your ancestor's regiment, allegiance, and rank. With these facts you can dig further into the database and bring up information on his unit.

If you find your ancestor in the Civil War Soldiers and Sailors database, you can sometimes learn more by accessing his complete compiled military service record. These can be ordered online through the National Archives. Alternatively, Footnote has digitized many of these files and placed them online where you can access them a bit cheaper and a lot quicker!

Once you've confirmed your ancestor's Civil War service you can often learn further details about him in pension records. If he lived long enough, the chances are good that your Union Civil War ancestor applied for a pension. If not, his widow or dependents likely applied. These federal pension records are available from the National Archives and can be ordered online. As previously mentioned, both Ancestry.com and Footnote offer subscription-based access to the general index of these Union pension files.

QUESTIONS?

Why aren't Confederate ancestors found in the National Archives?

Actually, the National Archives does hold the compiled military service records of Confederate officers and enlisted men, containing information taken from documents captured by Union forces and from Union prison and parole records. Because the Confederate States of America operated as a separate government, however, confederate pensions and bounty land were authorized by the individual Confederate or border states and the records are generally found in the respective state archives.

The federal government did not offer pensions to Confederate soldiers. Most Confederate states administered their own pension program, however. The veteran was eligible to apply for a pension to the state in which he lived, regardless of the unit in which he served. Generally, only indigent or disabled Confederate veterans, or their dependents, were eligible for pensions. The majority of these pension records can be found in the appropriate state archives, library, or historical society.

As with other genealogy records, a good search engine query such as *[your state] "civil war" genealogy* or *[your state] "civil war" records* will turn up a variety of useful databases and resources such as the Roster of Wisconsin Volunteers, War of the Rebellion, 1861–1865 (*www.wisconsinhistory.org/roster/index.html*), and the Texas State Library and Archives Commission Index to Confederate Civil War Pension Applications (*www.tsl.state.tx.us/arc/pensions/index.html*).

Research Twentieth-Century Conflicts

If you're new to tracing your family tree, you may not yet have gone back far enough to explore the rich records generated by the Civil War and American Revolution. That doesn't mean you can't benefit from military records, however. World Wars I and II, the Korean War, and the Vietnam War all generated records that are useful for genealogical research.

Was He Drafted?

Almost every male U.S. resident between the ages of eighteen and fortyfive completed a World War I Draft Registration Card in one of three separate draft registrations conducted in 1917 and 1918. These records include vital information on over 24 million men — whether native-born, naturalized, or alien — born between about 1873 and 1900. More than 80 percent of the men who registered for the draft never actually ended up serving in the military, so these can be a valuable resource for learning about your non-military ancestors as well.

Each of the registrations used a different form with a slight variation in the questions asked. All three include the individual's full name, home address, date of birth, age in years, and occupation; the name and address of his employer; his citizenship status; a physical description; the city; county; and state of the local draft board; the date of registration; and the signature of the applicant. The three registrations also included the following additional information:

1. June 5, 1917 (all men between the ages of twenty-one and thirty-one):Additional information included exact place of birth (usually including town), number of dependents, marital status, previous military service, and grounds for exemption.

2. June 5, 1918 (men who reached the age of twenty-one between June 5, 1917, and August 24, 1918): Additional information included exact place of birth, nearest relative's name and address, and father's birthplace.

3. September 12, 1918 (all men aged eighteen to forty-five who hadn't previously registered): No birthplace this time, but did ask for the name and address of the nearest relative.

The original World War I draft registration records are housed at the National Archives — Southeast Region near Atlanta, Georgia. The records have also been microfilmed and can be accessed through the Family History Library. Fully indexed, digitized copies of the original World War I draft registration cards can be accessed online as part of the subscription-based offerings at Ancestry.com. Alternatively, you can request scanned reproductions of the World War I draft registration cards online through the National Archives Order Online! service (*www.archives.gov/research/order/orderonline.html*).

ESSENTIALS

Soldiers, sailors, and marines aren't the only ones with wartime memories. Your family history should also consider the ancestors who lived through the wars as well, not just those who fought. Talk to your living relatives, read firsthand accounts and memoirs, and research the area where your ancestors lived for a firsthand perspective of life during wartime.

World War II draft records also exist, but registration cards from the Fourth Registration are the only ones currently available to the public due to privacy restrictions. This registration, often referred to as the "old man's registration," was conducted on April 27, 1942, and registered men who were born on or between April 28, 1877, and February 16, 1897, and not already in the military. The original draft cards are held by each state's National Archives regional branch, and are also available on microfilm from NARA or the Family History Library. Ancestry.com offers an online, searchable database of the currently available World War II draft registration cards. Unfortunately, the records for many of the southeastern states were destroyed before they were copied and will never be available. These include Alabama, Florida, Georgia, Kentucky, Mississippi, North Carolina, South Carolina, and Tennessee.

As useful as they are for locating information about ancestors who may have served in the military, World War I and World War II draft registration cards do not include any details of actual military service. For those men who did enlist in the military following their registration in either draft, you should turn to military service records for further information.

Request Your Ancestor's Military Service Record

Service records consist of the information that the government collects and keeps on any military personnel. This might include the soldier's enlistment/appointment, duty stations and assignments, training, performance, awards and medals, disciplinary actions, separation, discharge, and retirement. Military service records are available for enlisted men who served in the regular army throughout America's history, as well as discharged and deceased veterans of all services during the twentieth century.

Military records from just before World War I to the present are held in the National Military Personnel Records Center (NPRC) in St. Louis, Missouri. Access to many of these records is limited by privacy laws and, as such, they are not available online. Military veterans and the next of kin of deceased military veterans can order copies of these records through EVetRecs (*www.archives.gov/veterans/evetrecs/index.html*), an online military personnel records request system.

ALERT!

Don't overlook the most obvious source for twentieth century military information — the memories of your living relatives. Collect those one-of-a-kind war stories and memories from the people who lived them before it's too late. If your military ancestor is already deceased, talk to his siblings, spouse, or children.

Unfortunately, a disastrous fire at the NPRC on July 12, 1973, destroyed an estimated 16 to 18 million of these military personnel files. This includes approximately 80 percent of the U.S. Army personnel records for persons discharged between November 1, 1912, and January 1, 1960, and 75 percent of U.S. Air Force personnel records for persons discharged between September 25, 1947, and January 1, 1964, alphabetically through Hubbard, James E. These records were never duplicated or microfilmed prior to the fire, so there are no surviving copies. The NPRC will attempt to reconstruct a destroyed service record upon the request of a veteran or surviving family member.

Search Conflict-Specific Databases

A number of databases are available online for researching veterans of World War I, World War II, Korea, Vietnam, and other twentieth century conflicts. One of the largest is the World War II Army Enlistment Records File in NARA's Access to Archival Databases (*http://aad.archives.gov/aad*). This freely searchable database contains information on about 8.3 million men and women who enlisted in the U.S. Army during World War II. These records contain a great deal of useful information about the enlistee, including year and place of birth, civilian occupation, marital status, education, and enlistment details. For those who died during World War I, World War II, or the Korean War, the American Battle Monuments Commission (*www.abmc.gov*) maintains a variety of databases of Americans interred overseas, missing in action, or lost at sea.

Bone Up on Battle and Unit Histories

Don't end your search with your ancestor's military records. The Web shines at its best as a tool for historical background research, offering easy access to unit histories, battle details, firsthand accounts, photos, timelines, and memoirs. You can picture what military life was like for your ancestor by learning about the battles he participated in and the activities of his unit. Most people aren't lucky enough to have letters or a diary left behind by an ancestor, but the letters and journals of your ancestor's fellow soldiers may offer similar, although less personal, insight. If your ancestor was awarded a medal, buried in a military cemetery, or imprisoned in a POW camp, you can learn about that too. The Internet can also help you locate interactive maps, historical timelines, and photos of soldiers, ships, planes, and battlegrounds for enhancing your family history.

CHAPTER 10: A Nation of Immigrants

Virtually all Americans are descended from immigrants. Some arrived via the Bering Strait during prehistoric times. Europeans, mostly English, came during the seventeenth and eighteenth centuries to colonize and settle the rich new land. Still others fled famine and political unrest in northern and western Europe. Over 500,000 were brought unwillingly as slaves between 1619 and 1808. Millions more arrived by foot, car, bus, train, ship, and plane from all over the globe. All told, more than 50 million immigrants have been welcomed to the United States, so at some point your family tree will branch out beyond America's shores.

Find the Birthplace of Your Immigrant Ancestor

One of the biggest challenges in tracing your family history is locating information about immigrant ancestors. Because most foreign records are kept at the town level, discovering the name of your immigrant's town, county, or parish of origin is an important goal. Without this information, it will be very difficult to expand your research to your ancestor's native country.

Begin by learning as much as you can about that person. Talk to living family members and search through family possessions or histories for evidence of the family's origins. Are there any marriage records, death certificates, naturalization certificates, photographs, funeral cards, newspaper clippings, military records, or letters from relatives back in the old country? Was the family surname changed at some point in the past? What religion did the family practice and what church did they attend? Are there any other clues that family members can think of that may point to the family's origins?

If that doesn't provide the information you're looking for, turn your search to public records, including vital, tax, census, land, military, and probate records. Begin with your immigrant ancestor's death. Death certificates, probate records, obituaries, and tombstones may indicate a birthplace or, at least, a country of origin. If your ancestor died after about 1962, try a search in the Social Security Death Index (see Chapter 5). With the information from the index you can order a copy of the application he filled out when he applied for a social security card. These forms almost always give place of birth and names of parents.

After that, a good place to search for information on immigrant ancestors is in the federal census schedules. Begin with the most recent census in which your ancestor appeared and work your way back to 1850, or as far as you can. The 1900, 1910, 1920, and 1930 censuses each indicate the person's year of immigration to the United States and naturalization status ("Al" for alien, "Pa" for first papers, and "Na" for naturalized). These may help lead to passenger manifests or naturalization records for your immigrant ancestor. The 1850 to 1930 censuses indicate the person's state or country of birth, which can help narrow down your search. The 1880 to 1930 censuses also indicate the parents' birthplaces. Sometimes you get lucky and find a census-taker who writes in the town or county as well!

With the information you glean from census records you can often begin a search for your immigrant ancestor in passenger lists and naturalization records (discussed in detail later in this chapter). Early naturalization and passenger records generally only provide the country of birth, but more recent naturalization records and passenger records (after about 1906) will usually indicate the town of birth as well.

> World War I draft registration cards include details on approximately 24 million men in the United States who registered for the draft, and many include the place of birth. The first two (of three separate registrations), covering men born from about 1886 to 1897, asked for the date and location of birth, including the city or town as well as the state and country.

Plunge into Passenger Lists

Few achievements in family history research are as fulfilling as discovering your ancestor's name on a passenger list — often the first tangible evidence of their existence in America. If you've done your research on your immigrant ancestor, locating the actual manifest may tell you nothing new. But just seeing her name listed alongside those of her fellow passengers, and identifying the name of the ship she came over on, is a satisfying experience. And sometimes, especially with twentieth-century immigrants, the passenger list may provide that one clue you need to untangle your immigrant ancestor's story.

Most immigrants to the United States enter through a port city or bordercrossing checkpoint. If they entered legally and under normal circumstances, some type of paperwork was generally completed to document their entry. The content and thoroughness of this information varies by time period, and the immigration records that were generated can be classified into several broad categories.

Passenger Arrivals Prior to 1820

From early colonial times through 1819, documentation of passenger arrivals was under the jurisdiction of the colonies (and later, states). The primary concern of these entities was the taxation of goods, not the transport of passengers, and ships' captains were not always required to maintain passenger lists. Documentation of passengers from this time period may come from a variety of sources, including: a listing on the ship's cargo manifest, notation of passengers in the ship's log, publication of passenger arrivals in the local newspaper, and lists created upon departure from the country of origin. In addition, names of ship passengers may be noted in private journals, in the archives of immigrant-sponsoring societies or organizations, or even attached to medical reports for ships quarantined due to onboard disease.

Pennsylvania offers one notable exception to the lack of required passenger documentation prior to 1820. Beginning in 1727, Pennsylvania required that all non-British immigrants be identified and take an oath of allegiance. Generally only adult male passengers over the age of sixteen were recorded, although some of the later lists also include women and children. These early Pennsylvania lists, totaling about 65,000 passengers of primarily German and Swiss descent, were originally compiled in 1962 by Ralph B. Strassburger and William J. Hinke. The three-volume series of books titled *Pennsylvania German Pioneers* has since been reprinted. Some of the passenger lists from this series have been transcribed and made available online at Pennsylvania German Pioneers Passenger Lists (*http://freepages.genealogy.rootsweb.com/~pagermanpioneers*). Ancestry.com offers a searchable database of the entire series as part of its U.S. subscription package.

There is no central depository for pre-1820 passenger records, and many of them have been lost or destroyed. Those that remain are scattered in libraries, historical societies, archives, museums, and private hands. The majority of the known pre-1820 records have been published in books and journals. Two excellent bibliographic reference works detail many of these pre-1820 passenger records: Harold Lancour's *A Bibliography of Ship Passenger Lists, 1583–1825*, Third Edition, and William P. Filby's *Passenger and Immigration Lists Bibliography, 1538–1825*, Second Edition.

William Filby has also indexed many of these published pre-1820 passenger lists in his *Passenger and Immigration Lists Index*. This work, originally published in three volumes and supplemented annually, names about 2.25 million pre-1820 immigrants. It can be consulted in many major libraries and is also available online as part of the Immigration Collection at the subscription site Ancestry.com. Additional sources for online research of pre-1820 passenger lists can be found in genealogist Joe Beine's Bibliography of Books, CD-ROMs, and Online Databases for lists of U.S. passenger arrivals before 1820 (*http://home.att.net/~wee-monster/1820.html*).

Another online resource for early passenger lists is GenealogyBank.com. This subscription-based site also offers a free list of passengers who arrived in the United States from October 1, 1819, to September 30, 1820 (*www.genealogybank.com/free*), covering arrivals at thirty-four ports in fourteen states and the District of Columbia.

Customs Passenger Lists, 1820–1891

The federal government did not begin keeping a record of passenger arrivals until 1820, after Congress passed the Steerage Act of 1819. This act regulated the transport of passengers from foreign ports to the United States, and required ships' captains to submit a list of their ship's passengers to the customs collector at the port of entry. From January 1, 1820, to approximately 1891, these passenger lists were kept by the U.S. Customs Service and are thus often referred to as customs lists or customs passenger manifests. They generally provide a minimum amount of information on the immigrant, including:

- Name of the ship and its master
- Port of embarkation
- Date and port of arrival
- Passenger's name
- Passenger's age
- Passenger's gender
- Passenger's occupation
- Passenger's nationality

The U.S. Immigration Service Assumes Control in 1891

The number of immigrants entering the United States grew so quickly that Congress passed the first federal law regulating immigration in 1882. Nine years later, the Immigration Act of 1891 moved jurisdiction of the immigration process to the federal government, under the new Superintendent of Immigration (which became the Bureau of Immigration and Naturalization in 1906). This office was responsible for processing, admitting, and rejecting all immigrants seeking admission to the United States and for implementing national immigration policy.

QUESTIONS?

Could my ancestor's name have been changed at Ellis Island?

Many immigrants arriving in America did ultimately change their names, to avoid prejudice or to better assimilate into society. This name change most likely did not occur upon their arrival in the United States, however. It wasn't the job of Ellis Island and other port officials to write down names. Instead, they checked the immigrant's paperwork against the passenger list created by the shipping company at the port of departure, not the port of arrival.

As part of this implementation, "immigrant inspectors" were stationed at major American ports of entry for the purpose of collecting and reviewing the arrival manifests, referred to as immigration manifests or immigration passenger lists. These lists began to be recorded in about 1891 and continued until 1957, the exception being the port of Philadelphia, whose immigration passenger lists began in 1882. Although "Customs Passenger Lists" became "Immigration Passenger Lists," the information included on the two lists is virtually identical until 1893. Beginning that year, the federal government issued new standard forms with sixteen additional columns of information. Later revisions added even more information. These post-1892 passenger lists include the same information found on the earlier lists, along with the following additional details:

- Marital status

- Last town of residence

- Final destination in the United States, often including name of relative or friend

- Whether the passenger could read and write

- Amount of money the passenger was carrying

- Passenger's state of health

- Race (from 1903)

- Place of birth (from 1906)

- Personal description (from 1906)

- Name and address of nearest friend or relative in the old country (from 1907)

As with almost any rule, there are a few exceptions. One French immigrant's arrival in the United States is recorded on a 1946 passenger list, but the list itself provides none of the information you might expect for an immigrant at that time — listing only her name, age, and an application number. This is because she is listed along with over 800 other women and their children on that ship as "applying for admission to the United States under the Act of December 28, 1945." The War Brides act, which helped facilitate admission into the United States for foreign-born spouses of U.S. soldiers who married overseas during World War II, is just one of many such exceptions that may impact the information you'll find recorded on a passenger list.

ALERT!

If your ancestors arrived in the United States between 1892 and 1924, the probability is very high that they passed through Ellis Island, as it was the principal clearing point for immigrants arriving in the United States during that time. If you don't find your ancestor at Ellis Island, expand your search to other possible ports, considering where she first settled after she arrived.

Keep in mind as you research that passenger records are not always available for all ports during all time periods. The port of Galveston, Texas, for example, lost the majority of its immigration records from the years 1871 to 1894 in the great Galveston Hurricane of 1900. The National Archives holds a few extant passenger lists for San Francisco, but the official lists for that port were destroyed by fire in 1851 and 1940. Don't let this keep you from searching, however! Sometimes you'll find your ancestor immigrating through a port other than the one you expect, or you may find an alternate resource (such as an outbound passenger list from the departure city) that lists your ancestor. Online immigration indexes make searching much easier than it used to be, often allowing you to search across records of multiple ports in one step.

Locate Passenger Records Online

The National Archives is the primary repository for immigration records for passengers arriving from foreign ports between approximately 1820 and 1982. Microfilm copies of the passenger lists up to about 1960 are available at the National Archives building in Washington, D.C. Some are also available at NARA's regional branch facilities, and most of the microfilms can be borrowed through your local Family History Center. Just a few years ago, this was the only feasible method for doing research in passenger lists. Now, however, the majority of U.S. passenger records prior to about 1960 are also available for online research through a variety of sources.

One of the first large collections of passenger records to go online was the Ellis Island database (*www.ellisislandrecords.org*), which includes transcripts and digital images for arrivals at Ellis Island and the Port of New York between 1892 and 1924. The immigration passenger lists prior to 1897 for the Port of New York were actually destroyed in an 1897 fire at Ellis Island, but the customs passenger lists that were also kept for those years do survive and are included in the Ellis Island database. This free, searchable database includes approximately 22 million total records, along with ship photos and stories of the immigrant experience.

The "other" major New York port, Castle Garden, served as America's first official immigrant receiving station from 1855 through 1890, before being succeeded by Ellis Island in 1892. The Castle Garden Web site (*www.castlegarden.org*) offers a free searchable database of 10 million of the passengers who arrived at Castle Garden. These are transcriptions only, but Ancestry.com subscribers can access digital copies of the Castle Garden manifests.

The subscription-based U.S. Immigration Collection at Ancestry.com (*www.ancestry.com*) is the largest online source for passenger lists, including digital copies of virtually all readily available U.S. passenger lists from 1820 to 1960, as well as an index to the more than 75 million passenger names and 26 million crew names found on these lists. Nearly 80 percent of these records come from the receiving stations at the port of New York — primarily Ellis Island (including arrivals during years not included in the free Ellis Island database discussed previously). The major ports of Boston, San Francisco, New Orleans, Philadelphia, and Baltimore are also represented in this collection, along with more than 100 other U.S. ports of arrival. The records are available only to subscribers, or through a free trial offer.

Some of the other immigration databases and passenger lists that can be found online include:

- **Immigrant Ship Transcribers Guild** (*www.immigrantships.net*) — This site offers free access to more than 8,000 individual passenger manifests transcribed by volunteers. Click on the Passenger Lists and Special lists links to view and search the available records.

- **National Archives** (*http://aad.archives.gov/aad*) — The Access to Archival Databases (AAD) includes in their Passenger Lists a searchable database titled Passengers Who Arrived at the Port of New York During the Irish Famine, documenting primarily Irish immigrant arrivals during the period January 12, 1846, to December 31, 1851. About 70 percent of the passenger records list Ireland as the native country.

- **Galveston Immigration Database** (*www.galvestonhistory.org/Galveston_Immigration_Database.asp*) — Over 130,000 passengers who disembarked at the Port of Galveston between 1846 and 1948 are included in this free, searchable database. Not included are data on arrivals between the years 1871 and 1894, along with a few during 1900 because of the destruction of records in the 1900 hurricane.

- **Immigrant Servants Database**
 (*www.immigrantservants.com*) — A free online database of information on indentured servants, redemptioners, and transported convicts who settled south of New England between 1607 and 1820. Drawn from a variety of original sources in both America and Europe.

Many individuals who were ultimately bound for the United States first immigrated into Canada. There are many immigration lists and databases available online for entry into Canadian ports, including those at inGeneas (*www.ingeneas.com*) and the National Archives of Canada (*www.collectionscanada.gc.ca*).

Emigration (Outbound) Lists

Your ancestor most likely also left records behind in the old country when she came to the United States. These emigrant records created in the country of departure might include outbound passenger lists, visa or passport applications, or police emigrant records.

U.K. Outbound Passenger Lists 1890–1960

www.ancestorsonboard.com
The U.K. National Archives in association with Findmypast.com has created a searchable database featuring passenger lists for long-distance ships departing the British Isles between 1890 and 1960. Images of the passenger lists are available to download, view, save and print. Searching is free; transcriptions and images of the passenger lists are available on a payper-view basis.

Hamburg Passenger Lists 1850–1934

www.ancestry.com

Between 1850 and 1939, Hamburg, Germany, served as the "Gateway to the World" for about 5 million European emigrants. An index to the existing Hamburg lists from 1890 to 1912 was initially created and placed online by the Hamburg State Archives, but was later moved to the subscription-based site Ancestry.com. Ancestry's immigration collection also includes digitized copies of the passenger lists for ships that departed from Hamburg from 1850 to 1934 (with a gap from 1915 to 1919 due to World War I).

Bremen Passenger Lists 1920–1939

www.bremen-passengerlists.de

The majority of the passenger lists from the port of Bremen, Germany, were lost during World War II. This database offers access to the 3,017 passenger records that survived.

Danish Emigration Database

www.emiarch.dk

Emigration lists compiled by the Copenhagen Police from 1869 to 1908 have been transcribed and included in this free, searchable database. Information includes the name, last residence, age, year of emigration, and first destination of the emigrant from Denmark.

Norwegian Emigration Lists

http://digitalarkivet.uib.no

Click on English and then Database Selector to find data on emigrants that the National Archives of Norway extracted from ships' lists, police emigration records, and other sources, including digital images. Norway Heritage (*www.norwayheritage.com*) is another excellent source for information on emigrants from Norway.

ESSENTIALS

Passenger lists often include a variety of handwritten annotations — numbers, symbols, crossed-out names, etc. — that were added by immigration officials at the time of the ship's arrival, or later as part of a verification check. Sometimes these annotations may provide a clue to additional records, such as a naturalization certificate or warrant of arrest. Find explanations of these annotations online at About.com Genealogy (*http://genealogy.about.com/od/passenger_lists/a/annotations.htm*).

Border-Crossing Records — Canada and Mexico

Keeping records on alien arrivals at U.S. land borders was not required by early immigration acts. It wasn't until 1895 for Canada and about 1906 for Mexico that immigration authorities began to collect information on immigrants arriving in this manner. Separate card manifests were created for each individual that contain virtually the same information as that collected on a traditional ship passenger arrival manifest. These border-crossing records have been microfilmed and can be requested through any Family History Center. Online, Ancestry.com has an index and images of the records of aliens and citizens crossing into the United States from Canada via various ports of entry along the U.S.-Canadian border between 1895 and 1956.

E-LINK

No discussion of immigration research on the Web is complete without mentioning Steve Morse and his One-Step search tools. These search forms (www.stevemorse.org) provide powerful interfaces for searching popular existing genealogical databases, including major immigration and naturalization databases such as Ellis Island, Castle Garden, and the immigration databases at Ancestry.com.

The National Archives and Records Administration is currently processing microfilmed immigration records for individuals who crossed the U.S.-Mexican border between about 1903 and 1955 at land border ports in Arizona, California, New Mexico, and Texas. These are available for research through National Archives locations. Digital images of these records, along with a searchable index, are available online to subscribers at Ancestry.com.

Naturalization Records

Naturalization is the legal procedure by which an alien becomes a citizen of a country. Every nation has different rules that govern these requirements for citizenship. The records generated by the naturalization process can help you learn key information about your immigrant ancestor, including the place of birth and date, ship, and port of arrival. How much you can learn, however, will depend upon when and where the naturalization took place.

Congress passed the first law regulating naturalization in 1790. As a general rule, naturalization was a three-step process that took several years and generated a number of different documents:

1. First, the prospective citizen filed a *declaration of intent*, also referred to as *first papers*, to become a U.S. citizen, in which she renounced allegiance to foreign sovereignties. This document is signed by the immigrant.

2. Following a prescribed waiting period — generally two to five years — the immigrant could petition a federal court for formal citizenship. This did not have to occur in the same court in which she filed her declaration of intent. The application completed by the individual in this step is called the *petition for naturalization*.

3. After the petition was granted, a formal *certificate of citizenship* was issued to the petitioner.

Typically, the declaration provides more genealogically useful information than the petition. Prior to September 26, 1906, the declaration generally includes the name, country (but not town) of birth or allegiance, the date of the application, and the signature (if the individual being naturalized could write). Many included additional information, but the content varied dramatically from county to county, state to state, and year to year. Naturalizations after September 26, 1906, were handled on standardized forms, and include more detailed information such as the town of birth and the port and date of arrival.

As you can see, September 26, 1906, is a key date for naturalization research. Under the Basic Naturalization Act of 1906, naturalization forms became standardized and were forwarded to the newly formed U.S. Bureau of Naturalization for examination. Copies of all naturalizations after that date are in the custody of U.S. Citizenship and Immigration Services (*www.uscisw.gov*), which makes them easy to locate when you don't know where your ancestor was naturalized. Those more than fifty years old can be ordered from and retrieved by USCIS based on name, date of birth, and place of birth. These naturalization certificate files, known as C-files, generally contain a copy of the *declaration of intent* (to 1952), the petition for naturalization, and the certificate of naturalization. Occasionally, C-files also contain additional documents or correspondence.

Prior to September 26, 1906, an alien could be naturalized in any court of record — including courts at the local, county, state, or federal level — and the naturalization documents are usually found maintained among the court's records. Often it was a matter of the alien choosing to travel to the most conveniently located court with the authority to naturalize, so you may want to begin your search by identifying the courts closest to the place your ancestor lived at the approximate time she was naturalized. Remember, the approximate year of naturalization can be found on the 1920 census if your ancestor was living at that time.

Some naturalization indexes and records can be found online. Footnote is an excellent source, with digitized indexes and naturalization records for several U.S. states, including Maryland, Massachusetts, Pennsylvania, New York, and (Southern) California. For naturalization records found on various archives and personal sites, Joe Beine comes to the rescue with his list of Online Searchable Naturalization Indexes and Records (*http://home.att.net/~wee-monster/naturalization.html*).

Were They Eligible, or an Exception?

During certain points in American history, a variety of men, women, and children either were eligible to skip a few steps in the naturalization process or were granted automatic citizenship based on eligibility. Minor children, for example, were automatically granted citizenship upon the naturalization of their father. For a time (1855 to 1922), a woman could also achieve automatic citizenship either by marrying a citizen or upon the naturalization of her husband. Conversely, between 1907 and 1922, an American citizen woman could also lose her citizenship by marrying a man who was a foreign national, even if she never left the United States. From 1824 to 1906, minors who had lived in the United States at least five years before their twenty-third birthday (including those whose parents were not naturalized) were able to skip the Declaration step, as were individuals who served in the U.S. armies (Union forces) during the Civil War.

Racial requirements also affected eligibility for naturalization as a U.S. citizen. The naturalization process was first opened to people of African descent on July 14, 1870. Native Americans born outside the United States were barred from citizenship on racial grounds until 1940. The Chinese were the first Asians to gain the right to naturalization, in 1943; most had to wait until 1952, when the racial requirement was stricken from U.S. immigration law.

ALERT!

For detailed assistance in navigating the maze of available passenger records and locations, turn to the book *They Came in Ships: Finding Your Immigrant Ancestor's Arrival Record*, Third Edition, by John P. Colletta, Ph.D.. *They*

Became Americans: Finding Naturalization Records and Ethnic Origins by Loretto D. Szucs suggests a variety of ways to find naturalization records, as well as alternative sources for finding immigrant origins, and includes scores of document examples.

Not All Aliens Were Naturalized

Aliens living in the United States were not required to become citizens and, during the nineteenth century, it really gained them little other than the right to vote. Alien residents could legally buy and sell property, hold a job, and get married without citizenship status. For this reason, many nineteenth-and early-twentieth-century immigrants — at least 25 percent according to answers recorded in the 1890 through 1930 censuses — lived most of their lives in the United States as aliens and either never began or never completed the process of naturalization.

If censuses or other records lead you to believe that your ancestor never pursued naturalization, don't despair. Alien registration and visa records are often similarly rich in genealogical details. Information was collected on non-citizen residents of the United States at various points during American history, including special wartime registrations of alien citizens of "enemy" countries and a nationwide registration effort in the 1940s. Beginning in 1924, aliens arriving in the United States were required to apply for immigrant visas, which offer yet another source for information on foreignborn residents.

The Immigration Act of 1924 prompted a major change in U.S. immigration. Beginning July 1 of that year, everyone arriving at a U.S. port of entry was required to present some type of entry document. This might include a birth record or naturalization certificate for U.S. citizens, a re-entry permit for alien residents of the United States, or an immigrant visa or other paperwork for noncitizens. Prospective immigrants wishing to settle in the United States were required to apply for an immigrant visa at a U.S. embassy abroad. Those traveling to the United States for a temporary purpose such as a visit, or to attend school, applied for a nonimmigrant visa.

ESSENTIALS

U.S. Citizenship and Immigration Services (USCIS) (www.uscis.gov) holds most of the twentieth-century records discussed in this chapter, including naturalization files (after 1906), immigrant visa files, alien registration forms, and alien files. Copies of these records can be requested for your deceased relatives under the provisions of the Freedom of Information Act (FOIA), although USCIS plans to establish a fee-based genealogy program for requests for certain older records.

Fears of unknown enemies living within the United States prompted registration of resident aliens during wartime. These *enemy alien registration records* covered aliens who were living in the United States and were citizens of a country against which the United States had declared war.

The first such large-scale effort was prompted by World War I, when from November 1917 to April 1918 all resident, non-naturalized "enemy" aliens, including their American-born wives, if applicable, were required to register with the U.S. Marshal in their county of residence as a national security measure. These alien registration forms documented Germans, Italians, and citizens of other Axis powers living in the United States, including the date and ship of arrival, children's names and birth dates, parents' names and address, whether the alien was sympathetic to the enemy, names of relatives serving in the enemy forces, occupation and employer, a physical description, and a photograph and full set of fingerprints.

The majority of the World War I enemy alien records were destroyed in the 1920s by authority of Congress, but state and local copies of records for Kansas, Minnesota, Missouri, and the Phoenix, Arizona area, as well as a few scattered other registrations, still survive. Selected records can be found online, such as this index to Enemy Alien Registration Affidavits, 1917–1921 of Kansas (*http://skyways.lib.ks.us/genweb/kcgs/alienbyco.htm*).

The Alien Registration Act of 1940 required all alien residents age fourteen and older to register with the U.S. government and be fingerprinted. Aliens entering the country registered as they applied for admission. This alien registration requirement applied to all aliens over the age of fourteen, regardless of their nationality and immigration status. Millions of the aliens who registered had already lived in the United States for many years.

Alien registrations completed between July 1940 and April 1944 were microfilmed and placed in the custody of U.S. Citizenship and Immigration Services. These records are searchable by name, date of birth, and place of birth, and copies may be obtained through a Freedom of Information Act (FOIA) request.

Ethnic Research

Ethnic heritage is more than just a source of pride. It also offers alternative research strategies and resources for tracing your family tree. Different ethnic groups, both in the United States and abroad, preserve and maintain a variety of records of interest to genealogists. If you take time to become familiar with and explore these resources, you may learn something new about your own family heritage.

A variety of societies and organizations have been formed to collect, disseminate, and preserve the records and heritage of specific ethnic groups. These groups can often point you to specific records of interest for researching your ethnic ancestors. To locate such societies, look through the comprehensive directory of the Federation of Genealogical Societies Society Hall (*www.familyhistory.com/societyhall*).

Whether you're researching African-American, French-Canadian, Jewish, Irish, Hispanic, or Native-American ancestry, a variety of specialized databases relating to most ethnic or religious groups can be found online. The National Archives maintains an excellent list of links to major Web sites for ethnic genealogy research (*www.archives.gov/genealogy/heritage*), as does Cyndi's List (*www.cyndislist.com/topical.htm* — look under Ethnic Groups and People).

Put It into Practice

William Park, a Philadelphia resident, was born in Ireland according to U.S. census and other records. The next step is to learn when he arrived in the United States, and the town or county of origin in Ireland. The best place is to begin by examining the U.S. census records, specifically the 1920 census since it asks for both the year of immigration and the year of naturalization. In William's case, the 1920 census gives his year of immigration as 1888 and the year of naturalization as 1895. The 1900 census also lists 1888 as the year he immigrated, although in 1910 he states it was in 1891. Still, that's only three years off, so it's a reasonable time frame in which you can search.

A search for *William Park* with an arrival year of *1888* and *Ireland* as the place of origin turns up a New York passenger manifest entry for a William Park of the right age, arriving on the *Ethiopia* in New York harbor on 24 April 1888. There's little detail on this passenger list to prove it is the correct William Park, although it is a good possibility.

Family papers uncovered a passport for William Park, so the next step was to search the U.S. Passport Application records online at Ancestry.com. A search for *william park* born *1868 +/– 2* years with a residence of *philadelphia* quickly turned up his application for a U.S. passport in 1920. The document provides his exact date of birth (although the year varies from that given in other records by as much as five years) and that he was born in Donegal, Ireland. It also states his wife's name (Jane) and date of birth (26 Oct 1870), his father's name (Robert Park), and that he arrived in the United States on a ship sailing from Londonderry on 12 April 1888 (yes, this is the *Ethiopia*, providing confirmation that the right passenger arrival record was found). The application also gives the address where he was residing in 1920, his occupation (watchman), a physical description, and a photo of William and his wife Jane. What a great bunch of clues!

Because a passport application generally indicates overseas travel, another search for passenger records is in order. A search for William Park in Ancestry.com's passenger arrival records for 1920 turns up a match on the S.S. *Haverford* that sailed from Liverpool, England on 13 August 1920, arriving at the port of Philadelphia on the 26th of August. William and Jane Park are listed as passengers on page eighteen, with helpful information on their naturalization status; William Park was naturalized in the Court of Common Pleas, Philadelphia, in 1895, and his wife Jane Park is listed as naturalized "by marriage." Because they are U.S. citizens, little other information is provided outside of their ages and permanent residence.

Because the ship departed from Londonderry, England, it is likely that Ancestors on Board (*www.ancestorsonboard.com*) will have a copy of the corresponding outbound passenger list for *Haverford*, created as the ship departed England. Sure enough, they do — and it includes a very helpful piece of information, listing their address in Ireland as "C/O William Henry, Montober, Cookstown, Co. Tyrone, Ireland." Since William's wife's maiden name, is Jane Henry, this is likely the name and address of a relative they were visiting.

Additional searches of both Ancestry.com and Ancestors on Board for William Park (just to be sure nothing was missed) turned up another visit to Ireland in 1935, with a return on the *Caledonia* on 25 July 1935. The outbound list is especially helpful, giving the last address in the United Kingdom as "Devlinmore, Carrigart, Co. Donegal." Since it is known from previous research that William Park came from County Donegal, this provides a clue for further research.

The 1920 census says that William Park was naturalized in 1895 and he was a lifelong Philadelphia resident, so a stop at Footnote is a next good step as the site has digitized naturalization records for Pennsylvania. Unfortunately, no online naturalization record was found for William Park, most likely because he was naturalized in the Philadelphia Court of Common Pleas and Footnote's Pennsylvania naturalization records are from the U.S. Circuit Court. He does, however, appear as a witness on several other naturalization applications, including one for a Dell Park. Dill Park (the record was misindexed as "Dell") turns out to be living at the same address as William Park, and William Park is listed as a watchman — which matches the occupation he gave in census records. Looks like this might be a brother, or possibly a cousin, based on the birth year. More clues for you to pursue!

CHAPTER 11: Reach Out to Others

Discovering your roots can be a very personal journey, but it isn't something you'll easily accomplish alone. This is where the Internet truly offers an advantage for family history research, allowing you to easily connect and collaborate with other researchers. You can learn from and exchange data with others looking for similar information, discover previously unknown relatives, benefit from the experience and knowledge of others, or get help from individuals with access to records in far-off places. It's also really nice just to interact with other genealogists who share the same passion for family history that you do!

Make the Most of Boards and Lists

One of the easiest ways to connect with other researchers who may have information on your family is through genealogy-specific message boards and mailing lists. These serve as a prominent means of communication between family historians on the Internet, and allow for a tremendous amount of research sharing. Best of all, they're free and convenient. Most even allow you to search through archived postings, and some offer e-mail notification when a new query is posted that matches your surname or region of interest.

Join a Genealogy Mailing List

You can learn a lot by joining a mailing list focused on the surname, topic, or region on which your research is focused. Subscribing is as simple as sending an e-mail to the list administrator. Once you've joined, you'll receive copies of all e-mails sent to the list by other subscribing members, and can send your own messages that will be received by everyone on the list.

ESSENTIALS

A free Gmail e-mail account *(www.gmail.com)* is a good option for subscribing to mailing lists because Gmail elegantly combines all replies to a specific e-mail or topic into a single thread, or "conversation." The original e-mail and all replies are combined on one page, allowing lengthy mailing list conversations to take up only one line in your inbox. And when a conversation thread just keeps on going, Gmail even offers a mute button.

Most genealogy mailing lists offer two subscription modes:

- **List Mode** — You'll receive each message posted to the mailing list individually as it is sent (or after it is approved by the list moderator).

- **Digest Mode** — You'll receive periodic e-mails (usually daily) with several mailing list messages appended together. This can be a great method for reducing clutter in your inbox, but this mode can make it harder to follow a specific conversation.

After you subscribe, you'll usually receive a welcome e-mail within a few hours. Be sure to save this e-mail, as it will generally include important information on list rules and how to unsubscribe.

ALERT!

Genealogy mailing lists are similar to a community or neighborhood in that they reflect the personalities of their subscribers. Some lists are friendly with a number of off-topic "chatty" posts, while others are more strictly moderated with no off-topic discussion allowed. When you first join a mailing list it is a good idea to "lurk" for a few days to get a feel for the list and its members before posting your first message.

No matter what your genealogy research interest, there is probably a mailing list that applies — from individual surnames (such as CRISP) to research in specific counties or areas (such as the very active Bristol_and_Somerset-L mailing list at RootsWeb) or topics that you might want to stay on top of (such as Genealogy DNA). The vast majority of genealogy-related mailing lists (more than 24,000) are hosted through RootsWeb (*lists.rootsweb.com*) on topics such as surnames and places, immigration, religion, prisons, and heraldry. Check out Gen-Newbie for beginner-level help on anything from research to software. FamilySearch also offers free surname and subject-based mailing lists, known as collaboration e-mail lists (*www.familysearch.org/Eng/Share/Collaborate/frameset_share.asp*). You'll have to register to access this feature, but registration is free. Alternatively, you can use your favorite search engine to search for a mailing list on a particular topic, such as *genealogy "mailing list" "pitt county" nc*.

Delve into Genealogy Message Boards

Genealogy message boards and forums are different from mailing lists because messages are posted online, rather than sent to your e-mail address. Some message boards are open for anyone to browse and post to, while others require you to join for full access. As with mailing lists, they are free. The downside is that you have to remember to visit the message board periodically to find new messages, but most boards will at least send you an e-mail notification when someone responds to one of your postings and some will let you know whenever a new message is posted that matches your surname or area of interest. The upside is that message board postings will not clutter up your inbox like mailing lists do, so if you're short on time, message boards may be a good option for you. Because message board posts are archived online, most show up in Internet search engines. This increases the chances that your query for information on your greatgrandfather Charlie just might be found by someone with some answers.

Genealogy message boards and forums can be found in many locations online. The largest, most frequented boards are those at GenForum (*www.genforum.com*) and Ancestry.com (*http://boards.ancestry.com*). Although not a true message board, CousinConnect (*www.cousinconnect.com*) is another popular place for connecting with other researchers. It is dedicated solely to genealogical queries, and responses are sent directly to your e-mail.

Newsgroups, such as Yahoo! Groups (*http://groups.yahoo.com*) and Google Groups (*http://groups.google.com*), are similar to message boards, but they also incorporate the e-mail feature of mailing lists. In short, you get to choose whether you want new messages sent to you via e-mail or if you prefer to only read the new messages online. Many genealogical societies and genealogy research lists can be found on these sites.

Search the Archives

Message boards also allow you to search or browse through past posts, providing an excellent tool for connecting with other researchers. The Roots Web mailing lists are archived online as well (http://archiver.rootsweb.com), going all the way back to the beginning of the first genealogy mailing list, Roots-L, in 1987. Visit message boards and archived mailing lists for your primary surnames of interest and try searching for given names or locations from your family tree. Don't forget to search beyond the immediate family for spouses, cousins, siblings, and even neighbors. It's possible that people searching for those individuals may have information about your direct ancestors as well.

If you find a message you're interested in, even if it is an old one, take the time to reply with a brief message about the individual(s) you are researching and how you think they connect. This not only leaves a trail for the individual who originally posted the message, but may also catch the attention of others researching the same family. For tips on posting your own genealogy queries on message boards and mailing lists, see the "Ask the Right Way" section later in this chapter.

Ferret Out Family Trees

You probably wouldn't believe the number of people who think that genealogy is nothing more than a hunt for an already completed family tree. Since you're reading this book, you probably already realize that it doesn't work that way. But with millions of people becoming involved in researching their family history, large numbers of family trees *are* available on the Internet, and your chances of locating at least a portion of your family tree online are better than you might think.

Find Family Trees at FamilySearch

The FamilySearch Web site offers two different family tree databases for searching (*www.familysearch.org/Eng/Search/frameset_search.asp*), both containing information culled from pedigree charts and family trees submitted to the Family History Department of the Church of Jesus Christ of Latterday Saints. Ancestral File is the older of the two databases, created primarily from submissions gathered since 1979. Duplicate individuals from various contributors have been merged (not always correctly) and the only source information generally available for these family trees is the name of the submitter. Pedigree Resource File was created to overcome some of the deficiencies of Ancestral File, and includes notes and sources when provided by the contributor. These family trees are generally more recent, submitted by users to the FamilySearch Internet service. Only the index to the Pedigree Resource File can be searched online, however. For full access to a particular GEDCOM file, including source citations, you'll need to purchase the CD on which the GEDCOM is published. These are sold at cost, generally in sets of five, and can be purchased online. The new FamilySearch Family Tree (not yet publicly available at the time of this writing) will also feature usersubmitted family trees via a more user-friendly pedigree interface.

QUESTIONS?

How reliable is the information found in online family trees?

Many of the family trees submitted online are works in progress, and most probably contain at least an error or two. For this reason, you should never just download a family file you find online and add it directly to your own research without first taking some time to assess the accuracy of the information.

Member Trees at Ancestry.com

From the Ancestry home page (www.ancestry.com), click on the Family Trees tab to search for your ancestors in family trees submitted by members. (If you don't see a Family Trees tab, begin by clicking on Search in the navigation bar at the top, and then select Family Trees.) Search results will turn up family trees in a number of different collections, although Member Trees is their most current offering. Combined, the various family trees on Ancestry.com contain over 500 million names submitted by users. You can also submit to and search family trees through the free WorldConnect Web site (http://worldconnect.rootsweb.com) at RootsWeb.

GenCircles Global Tree

This is another popular database of lineage-linked family trees, contributed by users to the site (www.gencircles.com). Everyone can search and view the trees for free, but if you submit your own

GEDCOM file to GenCircles you can also take advantage of its SmartMatching technology to pair the people in your family tree file with other family trees in the database.

Take Your Search Global at GeneaNet.org

This pedigree database boasts more international family trees than most, and can be accessed in many languages as well. Because it was founded in France, GeneaNet (www.geneanet.org) is especially useful for searching family trees from France and other countries of continental Europe. There is a cost to upgrade to a Privilege Club membership, which offers enhanced search options and other features, but the family trees can all be searched and accessed free of charge. A handy e-mail alert can even notify you when new trees are added that match your criteria.

Search the Social Networks

Social networking sites offer yet another opportunity for connecting with others who may also be researching your ancestors. Popular social networks such as Facebook (www.facebook.com), MySpace (www.myspace.com), and Bebo (www.bebo.com) offer online family tree applications, such as FamilyBuilder (www.familybuilder.com), which allows their users to research and create family trees. In addition, there are also quite a few social networks dedicated primarily to family history and related topics. MyHeritage (www.myheritage.com), available in fifteen languages, is the largest and most widely used, with free online software for building your family tree, and smart matching technology to help you connect with others who may be researching the same relatives. Dozens of similar sites exist online, including GeneTree (www.genetree.com), Family Link (www.familylink.com), and Genes Reunited (www.genesreunited.co.uk). Most, though not all, of the genealogy-related social networking sites are free, although you'll often have to sign up as a member to search the family trees of other members.

Find Family Trees by Subscription

Genealogy is big business, and many companies make money by collecting and distributing family trees submitted by users. Genealogy.com, for example, offers WorldFamilyTree, a collection of family trees submitted by users of Family Tree Maker software and Genealogy.com. You can search these family trees online for free in Genealogy.com's Family Finder, but the family files (which include contact information for the contributor) are only available through online subscription or for purchase on CD-ROMs.

Ancestry.com offers free online searching of their online Member Trees, but full details from these trees can only be accessed by subscribers to Ancestry.com. Public Member Trees can be viewed by all Ancestry subscribers, while Personal Member Trees present only limited information online. Instead, you'll be offered the chance to connect with the person who submitted the family tree for further details through the Ancestry Connection Service — also only available to Ancestry.com subscribers.

In order to read and follow many of the family trees you'll find published online, it will help to have a basic understanding of the conventional numbering systems used by genealogists. Three of the most common include the Ahnentafel, a numbering system for ascending genealogies; and the Register System and NGS Quarterly System, used for descending genealogies. Examples and explanations of each system can be found online through a Google search.

In addition to the sites discussed here, there are dozens of other lineagelinked family tree databases to be found online, as well as thousands of individually created family trees published on personal Web sites across the Internet. Many can be found by entering a search such as *bumgardner family tree* in your favorite search engine.

Ask the Right Way

As you search the Web, you'll eventually come across other individuals researching the same ancestors. They may have information on your family that has been passed down to them, including treasured photographs, family stories, or even official documents and records. Or they may have researched a family line that you haven't yet had the time or resources to pursue. The first instinct — and generally a good one — is to contact them via e-mail. Keep in mind, however, that while your shared interest in the same ancestors means they are likely to be related to you in some distant way, in reality these people are basically strangers to you, as you are to them. To better ensure that your e-mail is opened and answered, or your message board post isn't overlooked, consider the following:

- **Include a meaningful subject line.** An e-mail from an unknown sender with a subject line of "Help!" is likely to be deleted without being read. Include the surname or full name of the individual you are writing about, as well as something like "genealogy" or "family history." Subject lines such as "Powell

Genealogy" or "Family Tree of Archibald Powell" are more likely to catch someone's attention than "Hi."

- **Keep it simple.** Explain briefly who you are and how you received the individual's name and e-mail address, as well as how you are related to the family you are contacting them about. Consider this first e-mail as an introduction to test the waters. It's not the best time to share your entire life story.

- **Be precise.** Many people throughout time have shared the same name, so you'll need to include additional details to help people identify the individual you're interested in. Where did he live? About when was he born? Can you provide names of other members of his family? Briefly explain what you already know or where you've already searched for this individual.

- **Don't ask for the moon.** A genealogist who has been patiently researching their family for years isn't really going to appreciate an e-mail asking for "everything you have on my family." Most genealogists are exceedingly generous in sharing the information they have uncovered, but be reasonable in what you ask for. Asking for a few specific facts, such as a marriage date or parents' names, is a good rule of thumb. They may offer to share more, of course, but they'll appreciate that you don't expect it of them.

- **Protect the privacy of the living.** While it's okay to share the names of your living relatives with other people, please don't give people their birth dates, social security numbers, or other private information.

- **Offer to share information in return.** If you're asking for something specific, it generally pays to offer something in return.

Perhaps you have some old family photos, documents, or dates that this individual may be interested in.

- **Say thank you.** Take a few minutes to respond with a quick note of thanks for any information or response you receive, whether it is truly helpful to you or not.

The above guidelines also apply to posting queries about your family online, whether on a genealogy forum or through a mailing list. Keep your query short and sweet, but include a relevant subject line, identifying details about your ancestor, and an overview of the places you've already searched.

ALERT!

A genealogist should always give credit where credit is due. Don't add someone else's family history research to your genealogy database and represent it as your own work, or share the information without acknowledging the source. The many careful, painstaking hours of research that went into putting all of those facts together deserve to be acknowledged.

Volunteer help can also be of tremendous assistance when researching your family tree. The genealogical community tends to be a very generous, giving group of individuals. All you have to do is ask a question and you'll usually get an answer. Help can be found almost anywhere you look, but the following groups are especially notable for the volunteer assistance they provide.

- **Books We Own** (*www.rootsweb.com/~bwo*): This free service has been around for more than a decade, connecting volunteers who own or have access to genealogy-related books and other published resources with people who need a quick lookup for their ancestor or a specific surname.

- **Random Acts of Genealogical Kindness** (*www.raogk.org*): More than 4,000 genealogists from all over the world volunteer their time to do everything from looking up a record at their local courthouse to taking pictures of a tombstone in a nearby cemetery. The time is donated freely, but you will be asked to cover any expenses.

Share Your Research

You can drastically improve your chances of connecting with other people researching your family line by making it easier for them to find you. Many people have connected with other branches of their family tree through an online Web site or community forum. Even the information posted through online obituary services and remembrance books has been known to bring families together.

One of the easiest ways to share your family history online is to upload a GEDCOM of your family history file to one or more of the lineage-linked databases previously discussed in this chapter. Your family tree doesn't need to be "finished" or even close to it, as long as what you do contribute has been well researched and you're comfortable with its accuracy. If your family tree is still very much a work in progress and you are unsure of some of your information, look for a service that allows you to easily add information or make corrections as your research progresses.

When creating your GEDCOM file for online publication, consider how much information you want to share online, and what you hope to achieve.

- It's always a good idea, of course, to remove personal information about living individuals before publishing your family tree online.

- Many people choose to include their sources, as this makes it easier for others to follow your research. Some family historians worry, however, that if they provide too much information people will just take and add it to their own family tree without contacting the researcher, which works against the point of putting the family tree online in the first place. To avoid this, some researchers choose to eliminate their sources from online family trees, and instead include a note asking anyone who is interested in further information to contact the researcher.

- If you like to use the Notes field of your genealogy software for everything from contact information to personal thoughts, stories, and questions concerning your relatives, it is best to leave that on your computer and not make it part of your online family tree. That generally falls under the category of "too much information."

E-LINK

The National Genealogical Society offers an excellent set of guidelines and standards for individuals wishing to improve their skills and performance in genealogy. Their "Standards for Sharing Information with Others" (*www.ngsgenealogy.org/comstandsharing.cfm*) discusses the responsibility of family historians when exchanging data, while the "Guidelines for Genealogical Self-Improvement and Growth" *(www.ngsgenealogy.org/comstandself.cfm)* provides recommendations concerning ongoing education in family history.

If you don't feel comfortable sharing your entire family tree online, there are other good options for reaching online researchers. One good way to connect with others who may be researching your family is to add your surnames to the RootsWeb Surname List (*http://rsl.rootsweb.com*), a free service that exists for the sole purpose of bringing researchers together. Over 1 million surnames are listed here, along with associated dates and locations where they are being researched. Each posting also includes the e-mail address of the person who submitted the surname so you can contact him or her directly. You can (and should) also post the surnames, dates, and locations that you're researching to the appropriate genealogy mailing lists and message boards discussed earlier in this chapter.

If you're creative and want to go beyond what most family tree databases offer, you may want to consider publishing your own family history Web site or blog. Publishing your family history online in this manner is discussed in more detail in Chapter 14.

Take a Class

Most people who take up a new hobby begin by buying a good beginner book or two or signing up for a class. You've already begun by reading this book, but if you're the type who likes more hands-on feedback, you might want to sign up for an online genealogy course. Prices vary from free to several hundred dollars, and the topics and lessons range from beginning research to advanced paleography or methodology. Most of the online genealogy courses are self-paced, and many offer quizzes, tests, and instructor feedback.

Get Started for Free

Several free beginner genealogy classes with enough information to get you through the basics of family tree research are available online through various Web sites. About.com Genealogy offers an Intro to Genealogy class (*http://genealogy.about.com/od/lessons*), with self-paced lessons and self-grading quizzes. Genealogy.com offers a series of tutorials (*www.genealogy.com/university.html*) created by several genealogists, covering topics ranging from beginner genealogy to immigrant origins. Additional online learning opportunities are available from RootsWeb's Guide to Tracing Family Trees (*www.rootsweb.com/~rwguide*) and Brigham Young University (*http://ce.byu.edu/is/site/courses/freecourses.cfm*), which offers over a dozen free mini genealogy tutorials online.

Learn from the National Genealogical Society (NGS)

In addition to their acclaimed home-study course, American Genealogy: A Basic Course, NGS offers several online courses (*u/edu.cfm*) including their Introduction to Genealogy course, two U.S. census courses, and a more in-depth course on Transcribing, Extracting, and Abstracting Genealogical Records. The online courses are self-paced, although they do have a six-month time limit, and offer a final self-grading exam upon completion. NGS members receive a member discount.

Enjoy an Online School Setting with GenClass

Experienced instructors at GenClass (*www.genclass.com*) offer a variety of four-week genealogy classes on topics ranging from Writing Your Family History to Scottish Genealogy. Each class is self-paced and includes a detailed course curriculum and optional online class meetings.

Earn College Credit or Enroll in a Certificate Program

A number of universities offer a variety of fee-based family history courses online. The National Institute for Genealogical Studies (*www.genealogicalstudies.com*), in association with the University of Toronto, offers a certificate of genealogical studies in American, Canadian, Scottish, Irish, and German records, as well as more general areas such as Genealogy Methodology and Librarianship. You can also elect to take classes purely for personal enrichment. In addition to its free classes, Brigham Young University offers several expanded low-fee genealogy courses through its Independent Study department (*http://ce.byu.edu/is/site/courses/freecourse.cfm*). Akamai University's distance-learning program offers an interdisciplinary Bachelor of Arts in Genealogical Studies (*www.akamaiuniversity.us/BachelorofArtsinGenealogicalStudies.html*).

To find even more genealogy classes, both fee-based and free, enter a phrase such as *online genealogy class* in an Internet search engine, or browse the listings at Cyndi's List (*www.cyndislist.com/educate.htm*) or About.com Genealogy (*http://genealogy.about.com/od/education*).

Connect with the Pros

As much fun as it can be to research your own family history, there can be times when it pays to turn to a professional for help. Maybe you just don't have the time to really dig into the records, or need some experienced assistance with putting all the pieces together. Or you might want to hire someone to do record lookups in a faraway city, or to take all of the bits and pieces of your research and turn them into a beautifully written family history. Sometimes you just need inside knowledge of local records, or a little extra help with a very stubborn problem.

Join a Society

Organizations such as lineage societies, genealogical societies, and patriotic organizations focus primarily on preserving the genealogy and family history of their members and region and making it available to the world. By joining such a society, you not only enjoy extra access to their records but can also benefit from the experience of the members. Most societies publish newsletters and quarterlies with record transcriptions, genealogy queries, articles on available records and resources, and news of interest to researchers. Many also offer some type of free or reduced-cost research benefits to their members, as well as the opportunity to include personal queries in their publications. Societies also generally arrange a variety of workshops, seminars, and research trips for their members. And, of course, there is the wonderful opportunity to network with other society members.

QUESTIONS?

Aren't genealogy conferences only for professionals?

Contrary to popular belief, genealogy conferences and institutes offer all genealogists — from the beginning hobbyist to the advanced professional — the opportunity to learn something new. They also offer the opportunity to learn from some of the world's best genealogists, keep up with new techniques and methodologies, and sample the latest software and gadgets. You can even take a genealogy cruise!

But what if the bulk of your research is not in your hometown? Do you join your local society? Or the society covering the area in which your ancestors lived? Both situations have their benefits. Many genealogists choose to belong to their local genealogical society despite having no ancestors from the area, for the chance to actively participate in the local genealogical community, in addition to joining societies in the areas where their ancestors lived. While you may not be able to attend the meetings or actively participate in the business of societies outside your area, membership still affords you the ability to keep up with the latest research news and resources through newsletters and quarterly publications. Many societies also operate mailing lists, so you can participate to an extent without leaving home.

Even if you choose not to join a genealogical society, most offer benefits to nonmembers as well. This often includes access to their library collection and a system for requesting research, lookups, and copies. Historical and genealogical societies are also good places to turn for inside information on records and repositories that will aid you in your research and for answers to your local research questions. They may have a Web site with searchable records, a forum for posting queries, or a mailing list that offers the opportunity to ask questions, request a lookup, or share the details of your family.

To find a genealogical or historical society near you, or that meets your research interests, visit the Society Hall (*www.familyhistory.com/societyhall*) operated by the Federation of Genealogical Societies and Ancestry.com. This site offers contact information on over 500 societies throughout the United States. Cyndi's List (*www.cyndislist.com/society.htm*) has several thousand links to societies and groups, organized alphabetically by the name of the society rather than geographically. You can also easily find many societies by entering a search such as *pennsylvania genealogical society* or *mennonite genealogy society* in your favorite search engine.

ESSENTIALS

Most genealogical and historical societies are nonprofit entities managed and run almost exclusively by volunteers. Despite the buzz over Internet genealogy, these groups are invaluable for their work in preserving our heritage for future generations. Yet the additional research opportunities offered by the Internet have left many societies facing declining membership, while operating costs continue to rise. By joining such a group, you help to keep them viable.

Hire a Professional

To locate a reputable genealogist for your project, it is best to turn to a professional association. These groups work to ensure quality and ethics among professional genealogists, which can offer you a certain element of confidence in the person you are hiring. Two organizations within the United States provide credentials or certification to genealogists from around the world who have passed rigorous tests of their research skills. The Board for Certification of Genealogists (BCG) (*www.bcgcertification.org*) offers research credentials as a Certified Genealogist (CG), as well as in a supplemental teaching category, Certified Genealogical Lecturer (CGL). A second credentialing organization, the International Commission for the Accreditation of Professional Genealogists (ICAPGen) (*www.icapgen.org*), also offers testing of genealogists worldwide through comprehensive written and oral examinations. They offer the designation of Accredited Genealogist (AG). The Association of Professional Genealogists (*www.apgenorg*) is another good place to turn when looking to hire a professional. This umbrella organization is not a credentialing body, but instead works to support high standards in the field of genealogy and requires all of its members to adhere to a code of ethics.

All three groups offer an online member list or database to assist you in locating a researcher by geographical location or specialty. Should you be dissatisfied with the work done by a member, each group also offers arbitration or other options to help in rectifying the situation.

CHAPTER 12: Dig Deeper

Genealogy can become addicting. As soon as you discover your ancestors' birth, death, and marriage dates, you may become enthralled with discovering more about them as people. But how do you dig deeper and get a more complete picture of who they were as people and what their lives may have been like? This chapter takes you through searching occupational records, finding family photos and postcards, delving into membership organizations, and even learning about your own DNA. There is always more to discover.

Books, Magazines, and Blogs

In Chapter 2, you were introduced to the thousands of family histories to be found in books, journals, and other printed publications. But these publications can be essential for their guidance as well. From them you can learn about new or unusual record sources, less-used repositories, and current genealogical standards.

E-LINK

Wondering what books you should purchase for your personal genealogy bookshelf? There are numerous articles and lists of suggestions available online, including "Top Five Genealogy Books for Beginners" *(http://genealogy.about.com/cs/beginnerscorner/tp/genealogy_books.htm)* and "What Reference Books Should I Own?" *(www.ancestry.com/learn /library/article.aspx?article=11934)*. The user reviews of genealogy books at Amazon *(www.amazon.com)* and Barnes & Noble *(www.bn.com)* can also help point you in the right direction.

Books

One such fundamental book for genealogists is *The Source, A Guidebook of American Genealogy*, Third Edition, by Loretto Dennis Szucs and Sandra Hargreaves Luebking, which covers record types in detail. This is a book that genealogists turn to again and again as they encounter new records or research situations. The second edition of *The Source* is also available online as a searchable database *(www.ancestry.com/search/db.aspx?dbid=3259)* for subscribers to Ancestry.com. Other very useful books in the same general category include Val Greenwood's *The Researcher's Guide to American Genealogy*, Third Edition; *The Handybook for Genealogists*, Eleventh Edition; and Ancestry's *Red Book: American State, County, and Town Sources*, Third Revised Edition, edited by Alice Eichholz, Ph.D. The latter is also searchable as an online database *(www.ancestry.com/search/db.aspx?dbid=3249)* at Ancestry.com. These books are such standards in the field that you'll generally find them at any library with a genealogy section.

Just about every professional genealogist subscribes to, or reads on a regular basis, one or more genealogical journals. These quality scholarly publications typically contain case studies, compiled genealogies, articles on new research methodologies, critical reviews of current books and software, and previously unpublished source materials. Some of the most widely read genealogical journals are the *National Genealogical Society Quarterly* (*www.ngsgenealogy.org*), the *New England Historical and Genealogical Register*(*www.newenglandancestors.org*), and *The American Genealogist* (*www.americangenealogist.com*). There are dozens of other excellent journals published by ethnic, state, and local societies. Subscriptions to these journals may be either part of or independent of a membership in the society. As an alternative to the traditional published journals, the Annals of Genealogical Research (*www.genlit.org*) offers an online forum for genealogists to publish compiled genealogies, case studies, and other scholarly genealogical articles with the same high standards as found in the published journals. Only a few articles are published here each year, but it's free.

Magazines

Popular genealogy magazines publish articles of more general interest, discussing record types, Web sites, new online databases, software, and upcoming genealogical events. For Internet genealogy, the aptly named *Internet Genealogy* magazine (*www.internet-genealogy.com*) focuses entirely on researching your family tree online. It highlights new genealogy Web sites, databases, and tools, as well as strategies for using those resources effectively. Also of interest to online researchers is the e-magazine *Digital Genealogist* (*www.digitalgenealogist.com*), which focuses on the use of technology in genealogy. You subscribe to this outstanding magazine just as you would a regular print magazine, but it comes to your e-mail six times a year as a PDF publication. Many of the traditional print genealogy magazines, most notably *Family Tree Magazine* (*www.familytreemagazine.com*) and *Ancestry Magazine* (*www.ancestry.com/learn/library/magazines/default.aspx*), include selected articles on their Web sites, as well as links to any online resources that were discussed.

Blogs

There are a lot of great genealogy blogs to choose from, and it's hard to select just a few to bring to your attention. Just about all genealogists have Dick Eastman's blog, Eastman's Online Genealogy Newsletter (*http://blog.eogn.com*), on their blogroll (list of links to other blogs). He's the one that genealogists expect to keep them up-to-date with the latest and greatest in genealogy tools, software, and online resources of interest to family historians. Leland Meitzler and the rest of the writers at Genealogy Blog (*www.genealogyblog.com*) also do a great job, commenting on news, current events, new Web sites and databases, and other items of interest to genealogists. Genea-Musings (*http://randysmusings.blogspot.com*), by Randy Seaver, is a pleasure to read because he updates almost daily, blogs on a wide variety of topics, and lets his passion for genealogy really shine through in his writing. Jasia will unleash your creative side with the thoughtful and inspiring posts on her Creative Genealogy blog (*http://creativegenealogy.blogspot.com*). You can find links to dozens more excellent genealogy blogs through Chris Dunham's Blog Finder (*http://blogfinder.genealogue.com*). There is definitely a lot of informative and inspiring writing going on out there in genealogy cyberspace, so go explore.

Occupational Records

Census records, marriage documents, obituary notices, and other sources of information on your ancestors will often make note of their occupation. This may seem like a trivial little detail, unnoticed in your quest for your ancestor's birth date or parents' names. Yet what your ancestors did for a living can tell you a great deal about them and what they found important in life. An individual's occupation may provide insight into his social status or place of origin. An occupation can also be used to distinguish between two individuals of the same name. Certain skilled occupations or trades, or even more unusual occupations, may have been passed down from father to son, providing indirect evidence of a family relationship. In short, an ancestor's choice of occupation can serve as a valuable guide marker in your path through their life.

Begin your search for occupational clues in your own home. Look closely at your old family photographs. Do you have any photos of your ancestor wearing a uniform, or standing in front of a family grocery store? Do the family papers contain any old business correspondence, pay stubs, farm or business ledgers, or retirement records? These may provide interesting information on your ancestor's work.

Other records previously covered in this book can also be excellent sources of occupational information. Census records from 1850 on record occupations for each individual. By 1920, this occupational information had expanded to include not only the occupation or trade, but also the type of business for which the individual worked and his occupational status (self-employed, salaried employee, or wage worker). City directories can also be an excellent source for occupations as they tend to list the name of the business, rather than just the type of work the ancestor did. They are also available for many more years than the federal census.

QUESTIONS?

My ancestor's occupation is not one that I recognize. What does it mean?

The world of work has changed greatly through the decades and centuries. For every new occupation — such as astronaut or Web designer — that is born, another occupation name or term — such as ripper (seller of fish) or pettifogger (a shyster lawyer) — has fallen into disuse. Type *old occupations* into your favorite search engine to find a number of helpful lists and glossaries.

Death records are another place where you'll often find occupational information. Death certificates and obituaries often list the individual's occupation or former occupation. If you can find your ancestor in the Social Security Death Index (SSDI), send for a copy of their SS-5 application record; it will include, among other things, their employer's name and address. Marriage records often include occupational information as well.

Once you identify your ancestor's occupation, the Internet is an excellent resource for learning more about the industry or profession in which he worked. If your great-great grandfather was a cordwainer (shoemaker), the Web site of the Honourable Cordwainer's Company (*www.thehcc.org*) offers a fascinating glimpse into the history of the profession, as well as a catalog of resources in the Guild's library and links to additional online resources on the occupation of shoemaking. If you hear of an ancestor who purportedly invented something, search the U.S. Patent and Trademark Office database (*www.uspto.gov/patft*) to see if he ever patented his invention. A variety of links to such occupation-oriented sites can be found on Cyndi's List: Occupations (*www.cyndislist.com/occupatn.htm*). An Internet search for a specific occupation can turn up interesting details. Unless the occupation was very specialized, you'll want to include other identifying details in your search as well, such as place, time period, or even ethnicity. For instance, a search on Google for *history farming north carolina* resulted in over 2 million hits. Narrowing the search further to *tobacco history pitt county north carolina* helps locate the interesting Pitt County Digital Tobacco History Exhibit (*http://digital.lib.ecu.edu/exhibits/tobacco/index.html*) with census records, business directories, warehouse maps, newspaper articles, and photos documenting the importance of the tobacco industry in the area around the turn of the twentieth century. Try a variety of different searches for your ancestor's occupation, and you may be surprised at all of the interesting information that turns up!

ESSENTIALS

Is your last name Barker, Cooper, Fuller, or Cohen? These and many other surnames originally derived from an individual's choice of occupation. A barker was a leather tanner. A cooper made barrels. The surname Cohen often derives from the Hebrew for "priest." And a fuller is someone who "fulled" or softened cloth by stretching, pounding, or walking on it.

State archives, local historical societies, and university libraries are also good places to look for information on various occupations as well as the records of businesses, institutions, and union and trade organizations. If the occupation was a common one in that particular area, such as with coal mining in Pennsylvania, you may find online exhibits with photos, documents, memoirs, and other valuable information. Most business and trade records will not be found online, however, but a search of online catalogs and manuscript collections can give you an idea of what is available offline, including membership lists, financial records, and occupational injury reports.

If the business, trade union, or other organization still exists, search the Internet for their Web site so you can contact them directly. They may be able to tell you what older records still exist and where they are stored. The U.S. Railroad Retirement Board (RRB) (*www.rrb.gov/mep/genealogy.asp*), for example, maintains records for individuals who worked in the rail industry after 1936, and their Web site includes information on how to request a search of those records for a fee. For railroad-working ancestors whose records aren't found with the RRB, the next step is to search for the records of the railroad companies themselves, most of which have been deposited with railroad museums and various historical societies. Again, the RRB comes to the rescue, with a list of depositories known to have railroad records.

Membership Organizations

Many societies, associations, and organizations are in some way committed to preserving the shared history of their members. This might include the history and heritage of a business or occupation, a geographical region or time period, or even a military unit or engagement. Personal information found in the records of these organizations might include full name, dates of admission and membership, and the name of a sponsor. Because many fraternal societies offered some type of death benefit, you may also find the date of death, an obituary or funeral notice, and a notice of funerary benefits to family members.

The number of societies that your ancestors may have joined is vast, and includes ethnic, religious, charitable, political, fraternal, and social organizations. Most were formed for mutual benefit and protection purposes:to organize group medical care and life insurance, locate and obtain jobs for members, preserve the values of the members' homeland, or assist with assimilation into the New World. All offered a place for camaraderie and brotherhood. For these reasons, membership societies were especially important among immigrants, offering a sense of community identity while assisting with their transition into the larger American society.

Fraternal and benevolent organizations in America reached their zenith of popularity during the late nineteenth century, with an estimated one in five males belonging to at least one fraternal order. The Freemasons and the Odd Fellows were the two largest societies, each with nearly a million members. The Order of Patrons of Husbandry, more commonly known as the Grange, also attracted a large following.

Lineage and hereditary societies, such as the Daughters of the American Revolution, have also been popular since the late nineteenth century. These societies each commemorate a different group of individuals, such as those who fought in the Civil War, or the first colonists to settle a particular area, and generally restrict their membership to individuals who can prove lineal descent from a qualifying ancestor.

ALERT!

An unusual symbol on your ancestor's tombstone may indicate membership in a fraternal organization. A shield, helmet, or the letters "KP" or "K of P" may indicate membership in the Order of Knights of Pythias. The compass and square is a Masonic symbol commonly found on tombstones. A grave marker in the shape of a tree or tree stump often indicates a member of Woodmen of the World.

Many lineage societies maintain active libraries and publish a periodical or newspaper for their members. Because membership in a lineage society generally requires documented evidence of descent from a specific qualifying individual, you can often glean significant genealogical information from its files. This might include membership application papers, pedigrees, and supporting evidence, such as pages from the family bible, birth and death certificates, or military documents.

Clues that your ancestor belonged to a membership society can be found in many sources, including obituaries, tombstones, local histories, biographies, and family memorabilia. If you know or suspect that your ancestor belonged to a particular organization, the next step is to learn where those records might be located. Most fraternal organizations, lineage societies, and other associations do not have their records computerized or provide them online. You'll often have to contact them via e-mail, fax, or snail mail to obtain the information you seek. Contact information for such organizations can often be found online through a Google search.

Web sites for many of the currently active fraternal societies are linked to from the National Fraternal Congress of America (*www.nfcanet.org*). The Societies and Groups section (*www.cyndislist.com/soc-gen.htm*) at Cyndi's List also offers thousands of links to ethnic and fraternal organizations, lineage societies, family associations, and other online societies and groups. Some organization Web sites, such as the Independent Order of

Odd Fellows (*www.ioof.org/family_research.htm*) and the Grand Army of the Republic Museum and Library (*www.garmuslib.org*), offer information on how to conduct family history research in their records. A small number of transcribed rosters, bylaws, histories, proceedings, and other records from a variety of fraternal organizations are part of the online database at Family Tree Connection (*www.familytreeconnection.com/records/fraternal.html*). Searching is free, but a subscription is required for full access.

ESSENTIALS

Family organizations — groups of people who are descended from a single individual or are gathering information about all individuals with a particular surname — can be a good source for family history information, but not all of them are online. Try *Directory of Family Associations*, Fourth Edition, by Elizabeth P. Bentley and Deborah Ann Carl, to help you locate active associations.

Photos and Postcards

After spending hours and hours reading and learning about ancestors in old records, you can't help but wonder how they must have looked. Do the visual images you have formed in your mind really have anything to do with how your ancestors looked in real life? Which one of them passed down the red hair that has shown up in your children or the hooked nose that appears at least once in every generation? How did they dress? What did their homes look like? Were they happy? Photographs of your ancestors can truly bring them to life.

A quest for family photographs should always begin with your family. Contact every relative you know to see what photos they have and are willing to share. Don't stop with your immediate relatives, either. When searching for family photos and memorabilia, it is essential to search out and contact all descendants of an ancestor. You never know which of the descendants of your great-grandfather's eighteen children might have possession of the family photo that used to hang over his mantel.

E-LINK

Postcards are another visual source of clues to your past, offering a glimpse into the towns, clothing styles, occupations, and day-to-day life of your ancestors. Auction sites such as eBay *(www.ebay.com)* are a great place to find vintage postcards. Images from more than 10,000 towns and cities can be found in the online Curt Teich Postcard Archives *(www.lcfpd.org/teich_archives)*. The Brooklyn Public Library hosts the collection "Historic Brooklyn Photographs" *(www.brooklynpubliclibrary.org/brooklyncollection/photo-collections.jsp)*.

If you encounter reluctance in a relative to let go of original photographs, offer to make copies of the pictures or pay to have copies made. If he doesn't want the photo removed from his home, you can often make a pretty good copy with a digital camera, or arrange to bring a laptop computer and a portable scanner.

Locate Photographs Online

If you're unable to obtain photos from your family members, it's time to turn to the Internet. There are literally millions of photographs posted online, and at least a few probably have some relevance to your family. Even if you can't locate a photograph of your ancestor, you may be able to find other photos of relevance, such as the town in which she lived, the place where she worked, or even her gravestone. Photo searches can also help turn up maps, scanned newspaper images, and other visual images of your family history.

Google Images search (*http://images.google.com*) is a great way to turn up ancestral photographs. Search for a specific surname, a town, or a cemetery to see what turns up. You may get really lucky and find a photograph of your ancestor, but Google Images search is also great for turning up tombstone photos, scenic town views, and photos of historic events. Just be sure to check the copyright and permissions for a photo if you plan to use it in your family genealogy.

A large number of online photographs are hidden away from search engines in digital photo collections, such as the Prints and Photographs collection of American Memory (*http://memory.loc.gov*) and the Francis Frith Collection (*www.francisfrith.com*) of over 100,000 photos from across Britain. Ancestry.com also has hundreds of thousands of family photos, submitted to Ancestry family trees by users, available for searching and viewing in its Public Member Photos database (*www.ancestry.com/search/db.aspx?dbid=1093*). Because they are in a database, the individual photos in such collections won't generally turn up in a standard Internet search. Instead, you have to search each collection individually. You can find many such historic photo collections (*http://genealogy.about.com/od/historic_photos*) listed on About.com Genealogy. Broad Internet searches such as *england photos* or *historic railroad photographs* can also help locate such collections.

ALERT!

County real estate or property Web sites are coming online every day to disseminate legal information on properties within the community. They are generally intended for tax and deed information, but many also include photos of the house or other property. This can be a neat way to find photos of older properties that used to be in your family. Look for links to Real Estate, Property Assessment, or Recorder of Deeds on the official county or city government site.

Another interesting source for family photographs online is what most genealogists call "orphan photos." These are photographs that have been found and rescued from flea markets, garage sales, and antique shops by thoughtful individuals, and placed online in the hope of reuniting them with a family member who will be glad to have them. Orphan photos can sometimes be found listed on genealogy message boards and mailing lists. There are also Web sites, such as Dead Fred (*www.deadfred.com*) and Ancient Faces (*www.ancientfaces.com/research*), devoted entirely to archiving mystery, orphan, and other family photos online.

Who Are Those People?

Great-aunt Mildred left you the family album, but it's full of unidentified photographs of people you've never seen before. How can you learn who those faces belong to and how they fit into your family tree? If you can safely remove the photos from the album, take them out carefully one by one to inspect the back for names, dates, notes, or a photographer's mark. Return each to the album immediately so you don't lose its position in the album or cause damage to the photo. If you plan to remove the photos from the album permanently, have your new storage solution handy so you can transfer the photos only once.

E-LINK

> Online digital photo-sharing services such as BubbleShare (*www.bubbleshare.com*) and Phanfare (*www.phanfare.com*) offer a great opportunity for collecting and sharing ancestral photographs, especially if you have a large extended family. Multiple family members can upload the photos from their collection. Everyone can view everyone else's photos, and add names, comments, and stories. Many services even let you add voice and video. Plus, everyone can download and make prints of their favorites!

Next, contact living family members to go through the album and write down whatever they can remember about each photo. If your relatives live far away, have digital copies made of the photos and send them to your relative on a CD-ROM or via e-mail. Anything they can remember may be helpful. If they don't know names, maybe they will at least know the branch of the family, recognize the backdrop, or be able to identify a single individual from a group photo. Have them look at items and props included in the photos as well.

Photos that remain unidentified can often be dated within a period of about a decade or so with a little detective work. By knowing the approximate date when the photograph was taken, you'll be more likely to identify possible names for the pictured individuals. Dozens of online tutorials can help you learn how to use clothing, jewelry, backdrops, photograph techniques, and other clues to identify the approximate date that a photo was taken. *Family Tree Magazine*, for example, offers a regular feature titled Identifying Family Photographs (*www.familytreemagazine.com/photos/previouscols.htm*) in which photo identification expert Maureen A. Taylor discusses photo-dating techniques using user-submitted photos as examples. Family Chronicle offers a brief online guide to Dating Early Photographs (*www.familychronicle.com/photoxtra.html*) with sample photographs organized by decade. They also offer two printed publications chock-full of reproductions of old photographs of known dates, offering numerous examples to compare with your own family photographs.

Save Your Family Photos Before It's Too Late!

Many family photographs, and the stories that go with them, are lost each year. Heat, humidity, and even bugs do their damage. Fire, flooding, and other disasters wipe out precious family memories. When there is a death in the family, relatives may divide up the photos, discarding the ones they don't want. Family photo albums and boxes of loose photos often end up sold with an estate or dumped in the trash. Almost every antique store has a section filled with old family photos, scrapbooks, and postcards — bits of family history that have been lost to anonymity.

If you have older relatives, consider letting them know that you would be happy to take care of their photos. If you want to make sure your photograph collection has a good home after you die, sit down and make sure all of the pictures are labeled (to the best of your ability), and make plans for a special family member to inherit the photos. If you have access to a digital scanner, or can afford to have a professional do the work for you, you may want to scan your ancestral photos into digital format and then burn them to CD or DVD for long-term storage and backup.

DNA and Genetic Genealogy

Clues to your past cannot only be found in the records at the library and courthouse, they can also be found in your genes. DNA has been used for many years to identify people, but in the year 2000, DNA testing for genealogical applications hit the commercial market. DNA testing is best used to help confirm a link where no conventional source records exist or, in some cases, to determine if a person is part of a larger group, such as the Jewish Cohanim lineage.

Genetic genealogy tests look at the variations in the sequence of DNA from one person to the next. The more closely two people are related, the more similar their genetic material, or genomes. What's interesting is that all humans are about 99.9 percent the same. It's in that other 0.1 percent that you find the genetic differences that makes you unique. Every once in a blue moon a small change or "stutter" occurs in this unique portion of our DNA. This "hiccup," or genetic mutation, is then passed down to a person's descendants. A similar mutation found in two people's DNA means that they share an ancestor somewhere in the past.

QUESTIONS?

Will genealogy DNA testing reveal medical problems?

The markers analyzed in traditional genealogy tests are from non-coding DNA, or what is commonly referred to as "junk DNA." These stretches of DNA have no known function and do not reveal anything about personal traits or medical conditions. Because genetic testing is so sensitive, most companies have strict policies in place to assure their clients that their DNA is kept private, and separate from any personally identifying information. Generally, most facilities assign a unique number to each DNA sample, and that number and the surname is all the testing lab ever sees.

To help locate these genetic mutations, scientists have identified genetic *markers*, certain short segments of the DNA strand with known genetic characteristics. These markers, which can be found at specific locations, (or loci), on the chromosome, are essentially places where the same pattern repeats a number of times. Since the number of repeats within these sequences is inherited, people who match at a number of markers are almost certain to share a common ancestor.

A special type of marker known as a Short Tandem Repeat (STR) is the one most often used in genealogy testing. In general, a DNA testing company will offer several different levels of tests — twelve markers, twenty five markers, thirty-seven markers, sixty-seven markers, and so on. Depending upon the number of markers tested and the number of matches, your results will also indicate with a certain degree of probability how long ago this common ancestor lived. It is best to test a minimum of twenty-five markers to achieve any sort of meaningful result. Basically, the more markers you test, the more conclusive your tests will be. The cost also goes up as the number of markers goes up, however, so most people choose to test a moderate number of markers (in the twenty-five to thirty-seven range). Almost all testing companies keep your DNA on file for a specified number of years, and will allow you to test additional markers at a future date if you so desire.

Genealogy DNA tests do NOT tell people precisely how they are related, or who their common ancestor is. DNA tests also can't tell you about the large portions of your family tree that don't descend directly from father to father, or mother to mother, unless you pair this with traditional genealogy research to track down direct-line descendants of those ancestors and have them participate in DNA testing.

For genetic genealogy purposes, two types of DNA can provide useful information: the Y chromosome and mtDNA (mitochondrial DNA).

Paternal Ancestry — Y-DNA

Human gender is determined by the X and Y chromosomes, two of the twenty-six chromosomes carried in the human cell. Females have two X chromosomes and males have one X and one Y chromosome. When a child is conceived, it receives one sex chromosome from each parent. The chromosome from the mother will always be X, but the chromosome from the father could be either X or Y. A child who receives an X chromosome from the father will be a girl; receiving a Y chromosome will make the child a boy.

Because the Y chromosome is the only human chromosome not affected by the constant reshuffling of parental genes, the DNA present in the Y chromosome is passed down virtually unchanged for many generations. This means that every male directly descended from the same distant male ancestor will have an extremely similar pattern of Y-DNA markers, making the Y chromosome extremely useful to genealogists. Since the Y chromosome is only present in males, the popular Y-DNA genealogy test can only be done on males, however. If you are a female interested in your paternal line, you will need to find a male relative (father, brother, cousin, etc.) from that line to be tested.

When you take a Y-line DNA test, your results will come back as a string of numbers. These numbers represent the repeats (stutters) found for each of the tested markers on the Y chromosome. These results have no real meaning taken on their own. Instead, you compare your results with other individuals to whom you think you are related to see how many of your markers match. Matching numbers at most or all of the tested markers can indicate a shared ancestor. Depending upon the number of exact matches, and the number of markers tested, you can also determine approximately how recently this common ancestor was likely to have lived (within five generations, sixteen generations, etc.).

E-LINK

Additional information and collaboration resources for genetic genealogy are available from several online sources. The International Society of Genetic Genealogy (*www.isogg.org*) exists to educate people about the use of genetics in genealogy through workshops, beginner tutorials, and an online forum. The Blair DNA Project (*http://blairgenealogy.com /dna/dna101.html*) offers an excellent introduction to genetics and DNA in lay terms.

Maternal Ancestry — Mitochondrial DNA

Just so the females don't feel left out, you have your own special DNA test as well. Maternal DNA, referred to as mitochondrial DNA or mtDNA, is passed down from mothers to their sons and daughters. It is only carried through the female line, however, so while a son inherits his mother's mtDNA, he does not pass it down to his own children. It does mean, how-ever, that both men and women can test their mtDNA.

The mtDNA mutates much more slowly than Y-DNA, so it is really only useful for determining distant ancestry. Your mtDNA results will generally be compared to a common reference sequence called the Cambridge Reference Sequence (CRS), to identify your specific haplotype, a set of closely linked alleles (variant forms of the same gene) that are inherited as a unit. People with the same haplotype share a common ancestor somewhere in the maternal line. This could be as recent as a few generations, or it could be dozens of generations back in the family tree. Your test results may also include your haplogroup, (basically a group of related haplotypes), which offers a link to the ancient lineage to which you belong.

While Y-DNA and mtDNA are the most common genetic tests for gene-alogy, there are also other tests available for determining distant and recent ethnic origins. These include Autosomal SNP (Single Nucleotide Polymorphism; pronounced "snip"), generally used in genealogy for determining general biogeographical origins, or the percentage of various population groups (African, European, etc.) that exist in your DNA; and X-STR DNA, which tests markers on the X chromosome. To learn more about the various DNA test types and what you can expect from the results, try the Genealogy-DNA-L mailing list (*http://lists.rootsweb.com/index/other/DNA/GENEALOGY-DNA.html*) at RootsWeb.com.

ESSENTIALS

A variety of DNA testing labs specialize in DNA testing for genealogy applications. FamilyTreeDNA (*www.familytreedna.com*) is the largest genetic genealogy testing company, with the largest online database of DNA records. If you're looking for a bargain, check out the National Geographic Society's Genographic Project (*www.nationalgeographic.com/genographic*). DNATribes (*www.dnatribes.com*) is a popular option for autosomal testing. Locate others with a Google search such as genealogy dna testing.

Use DNA Testing to Learn about Your Roots

DNA testing is easy and painless. Basically, you sign up with a DNA testing company and order the test in which you are interested. They will send you a kit with a cheek swab (or in some cases a mouthwash) with which to collect your sample. No blood is collected. You then send back the kit containing your DNA sample. A few weeks later you'll get your results.

Join a Surname Project

Genetic testing for ancestral connections provides the most information when you have others with whom to compare the results. One of the best ways to do this is to join a DNA surname study in which men with the same surname compare their lineages and DNA test results to see if they are related. Women can play too, of course, but they'll have to find a direct-line ancestor with the surname to take the actual DNA test, as surname studies are based on Y-line ancestry. As an added bonus, many testing facilities offer a substantial discount to participants in group projects.

Several thousand surname projects are already under way, offering an opportunity to quickly connect with other potential relatives. Many surname projects have their own Web site, so an Internet search such as *crane dna* or *crane surname study* may turn up just what you need. Be sure to search for variations of your surname as well (e.g., Crain, Craine, Crayne). For smaller or newly created projects, check the project listings at the various DNA testing companies. For example, DNA Heritage (www.dnaheritage.com) and FamilyTreeDNA (www.familytreedna.com) both offer links to surname projects from their home page. Lists of surname projects can also be found on Cyndi's List (www.cyndislist.com/surn-dna.htm).

Create a Medical Family Tree

Many health conditions, from cancer to high blood pressure, tend to run in families. Some of these diseases are purely genetic. Most, however, are a mixture of genetic makeup and environmental factors. In these cases, you are not born with the condition; you only inherit a susceptibility or predisposition to developing it during your lifetime. By tracing the health problems and diseases suffered by your parents, grandparents, and other blood relatives, you can learn about your possible inherited risks. This information can help you and your doctor take preventive steps to lessen your chances of acquiring the disease or condition.

The Internet offers a number of resources for anyone interested in tracing their medical family tree. Online tools and guidance are available, for example, on the Web site of the U.S. Surgeon General's Family History Initiative (*www.hhs.gov/familyhistory*).

If you have concerns about your family medical history, you may want to see a genetics specialist. To find genetics professionals in your area, search the online directories offered through the National Society of Genetic Counselors (*www.nsgc.org*), GeneClinics (*www.geneclinics.org*), and the American Society of Human Genetics (*www.ashg.org*). To find more information about the medical conditions present in your family and about support groups, try the Disease InfoSearch and Organization Search features offered by the Genetic Alliance (*www.geneticalliance.org*).

CHAPTER 13: Locate Records Abroad

America is truly a nation of immigrants, with the vast majority arriving during the past 150 years. In fact, 95 percent of Americans today have descended from individuals who did not live on this continent in the eighteenth century. That's a brief flicker in terms of world history. For you, this means it probably won't be long before your research leads you past America's borders.

A Nation of Immigrants

If you're worried that you don't have the skill for foreign research, don't be. The research skills and techniques that you already use readily transfer to research in a new location. Yes, there will be a few stumbling blocks, such as language barriers. You'll also need to spend time familiarizing yourself with the country's history, including changing political and geographical boundaries. But once you find that first ancestor in the "old country," you'll be hooked!

Limited space prevents going into extensive detail on genealogy research in countries around the world. Instead, this chapter takes a look at some of the major online family history resources available for each country, with links to Web sites where you can access further research guidance and resources on the countries where your ancestors once lived.

Canada

A large amount of genealogical and historical data for Canada is already available online, with more being added all the time. Most records are maintained at the province level, so you will need to have an idea of what part of Canada your ancestors came from before embarking on your research.

ALERT!

A free twenty-four-page guide entitled "Tracing Your Ancestors in Canada" is available for download in PDF format (*www.collectionscanada.gc.ca/genealogy/022-607.001-e.html*) from Library and Archives Canada. This guide describes the primary sources of genealogical information available in Library and Archives Canada as well as an overview of information in other Canadian centers.

Billing itself as a "gateway to Canadian genealogy," the CanadaGenWeb Project (*www.rootsweb.com/~canwgw*) is available in English and French with queries, lookups, and an FAQ. Besides links to province-specific resources, you'll discover a timeline of Canadian history, facts about famous Canadians, a cemetery transcription project, and a special Web site just for kids.

The Canadian Genealogy Centre (*www.collectionscanada.ca/genealogy/index-e.html*) of Library and Archives Canada has posted numerous (and free) online databases that are useful for anyone researching Canadian roots. Select Search for Ancestors to find the 1851, 1901, and 1911 censuses of

Canada; a variety of immigration records and passenger lists; naturalization records; land grants; and early marriage bonds for Upper and Lower Canada.

If you are having trouble locating your ancestor in the Canadian census images on the Library and Archives Canada site, head on over to Automated Genealogy (*www.automatedgenealogy.com*). Several genealogy projects are under development at this free, volunteer-supported Web site, including indexes of the 1901, 1906, and 1911 censuses of Canada.

QUESTIONS?

Where can I find Canadian records of birth, marriage, and death?

Civil registration of vital statistics in Canada is a provincial responsibility; available records and access will vary by province. Some archives and vital statistic offices, such as the British Columbia Archives, offer online indexes to historical birth, marriage, and death registrations. Others only provide information on how to order a certificate via mail. Try a search such as *canada vital records* or *alberta vital records* or *ontario marriages* to learn what's available in your area of interest.

A transcription of the complete 1881 Canadian census is online for free searching at FamilySearch (*www.familysearch.org*). Select the Search tab, then Census, to search this database for your Canadian ancestors.

The largest collection of Canadian family history records available online can be found on the subscription site Ancestry.ca (*www.ancestry.ca*). The fully searchable databases include indexes and images for the 1851, 1901, 1906, and 1911 censuses of Canada, along with Canadian immigrant records and Ontario birth, marriage, and death records. This is a companion site to the U.S.-based Ancestry.com and includes the same records, although a Canada Deluxe membership that only includes Canadian records is available exclusively on Ancestry.ca.

Find information on more than 116,000 Canadians and Newfoundlanders who fought and died while in service to Canada at the Canadian Virtual War Memorial (*www.vac-acc.gc.ca/remembers/sub.cfm?source=collections/virtualmem*).
Information in this free database includes the individual's military service number, unit and division, date of birth, and burial information. It also often includes that individual's hometown and the names of spouse and parents.

Since much of Canada's records are created and maintained at the provincial level, you'll want to check the archives, libraries, and other repositories in the province where your ancestors lived. The site That's My Family (*www.thatsmyfamily.info*) helps make this easy, offering a free online search interface for multiple databases from various provinces. Canadian Genealogy and History Links (*www.islandnet.com/~jveinot/cghl/archives.html*) is an excellent resource for Web links to provincial archives and libraries, as well as other resources for Canadian genealogy. You can also find a wealth of Canadian research guides and database links at Cyndi's List — Canada (*www.cyndislist.com/canada.htm*) and About.com Genealogy — Canada (*http://genealogy.about.com/od/canada*).

Mexico, Central America, and South America

The countries of Central and South America do not yet have many family history records available online. Yet you can still use the Internet to learn how to conduct research in these countries, and find contact information and instructions for ordering records. A few of the larger Web sites with data of interest to family historians are detailed below.

Find Births and Marriages at FamilySearch

Available for free searching via the FamilySearch Web site, the Mexico Vital Records Index (*www.familysearch.org*) includes 300,000 marriage and 1.9 million birth and christening records from Mexico, a partial listing of records covering the years 1659 to 1905. From the FamilySearch home page, click on Search and then select Vital Records from the left-hand navigation bar.

Are You Eligible for the Aztec Club of 1847?

This patriotic society welcomes members based on descent from a commissioned officer of the U.S. Army, Navy, or Marine Corps who served in any part of Mexico or adjacent waters during the Mexican War (1846–1848). The society's Web site (*www.aztecclub.com*) explains its history and membership requirements, offers information about the Mexican War, and provides access to bibliographies and a database of American Mexican War Officers.

E-LINK

Before you dig into the online databases, it pays to become familiar with the ins and outs of genealogy research in your country of interest. Introductory guides to research in many countries around the world can be found at FamilySearch.org *(www.familysearch.org)*. Select "Research Helps" (under the "Search" tab) and browse to your country of interest.

Locate Country-Specific Resources at GenWeb

Visit the North America Genealogy Project (*www.rootsweb.com/~nrthamgw*) to locate online resources and records, and to connect with fellow researchers for the countries of Central America, including Belize, Costa Rica, El Salvador, Guatemala, Honduras, Nicaragua, and Panama. For genealogy research in South America — encompassing the countries of Argentina, Brazil, Colombia, Chile, Peru, Venezuela, and others — the South AmericanGenWeb Project (*www.rootsweb.com/~sthamgw*) serves as an online repository for source records, family histories, genealogy queries, and links to online databases. Both sites are free, fully supported by volunteers.

British Isles

There is a vast wealth of data available for the regions that make up the British Isles — England, Scotland, Wales, Ireland, the Channel Islands, and the Isle of Man. There is, in fact, much more than can be adequately discussed in this book. But to get you started, here are some of the largest and most useful online resources for genealogy research in the British Isles.

Two of the best jumping-off points include GENUKI and the BritishIslesGenWeb. GENUKI (*www.genuki.org.uk*), short for

Genealogy of the United Kingdom and Ireland, serves as a virtual reference library of genealogical information with relevance to the United Kingdom and Ireland. It's a great place to look for links to vital Web sites and primary source documents organized by region, county, and topic. The BritishIslesGenWeb site (*www.britishislesgenweb.org*) has genealogical data and queries, along with links to the eleven British Isles country projects (Caribbean Islands, Channel Islands, England, Falkland Islands, Gibraltar, Ireland, Isle of Man, Northern Ireland, Scotland, St. Helena, and Wales). Don't miss their Location Finder — a useful tool for identifying the location of your ancestor's parish.

Once you've spent some time exploring the records and resources available at the above volunteer projects, it's time to jump into online records and databases.

If you're confused about the differences between the terms British, Great Britain, the United Kingdom, and the British Isles, you're not alone. It's important to learn the distinctions, however, because it not only affects how records are organized and where you will find them, but it will also prevent you from offending someone or appearing ignorant during the course of your research. Learn more from "What is British?" (*http://genealogy.about.com/b/a/255920.htm*).

Census Records

Like census records in the United States, censuses in most of the British Isles were conducted every ten years — but in the second year of the decade (the years ending in "1") instead of the first. Because they cover the entire population, they are among the most comprehensive records available online for research in this region.

The 1881 census of England and Wales is a good place to begin your census research, because it is accessible free of charge at FamilySearch. From there, make a stop at FreeCEN (*www.freecen.org.uk*), where volunteers worldwide are transcribing U.K. census records for 1841, 1851, 1861, 1871, and 1891. Coverage varies widely — with some counties and years almost 100 percent complete, and other counties with nothing. GENUKI, as well as Census Online (discussed in Chapter 6), are good places to find links to free census indexes, transcriptions, and images, organized by region and county.

ALERT!

The volunteer indexing project at the Genealogist offers rewards in the form of vouchers and subscriptions in return for time spent assisting in their transcription efforts. As a volunteer, you would participate in errorchecking previously indexed entries, using special online tools. If you have some free time to offer and would enjoy free database access in return, consider signing up as a volunteer at UKIndexer *(www.ukindexer.co.uk)*.

Once you've exhausted the free offerings, censuses from 1841 through 1901 (the most recent released to the public, with the exception of the 1911 Irish census) can be viewed on a variety of pay-per-view or subscription sites. Ancestry.com offers census indexes and images for all years in England, Wales, Scotland, the Channel Islands, and the Isle of Man as part of their World Records Collection subscription. The National Archives offers free online searches of the 1901 census of England and Wales (_www.1901censusonline.com_), although you'll have to pay to access full transcriptions and digital images. The official genealogy Web site of the Scottish government, ScotlandsPeople (_www.scotlandspeople.gov.uk_), offers subscription-based access to indexes and images of the Scottish census, for the years from 1841 to 1871 and 1891 to 1901, plus index and transcription (no images) of the 1881 census. FindMyPast (_www.findmypast.com_) offers a free census search and payper-view access to census transcriptions and images for the 1841, 1861, 1871, and 1891 census of England and Wales. This can save you a little money over the subscription-based sites if you're searching for only a few ancestors. The BMD Index (_www.bmdindex.co.uk_), powered by the Genealogist, offers inexpensive subscription access to transcripts and indices for the England and Wales census for all years, and images for 1841, 1851, 1861, 1871, and 1891. Another alternative for the 1841 census, which has a more accurate index than other offerings, is available at subscription-based BritishOrigins (_www.origins.net_).

Census records for Ireland are hard to find online. The 1861, 1871, 1881, and 1891 census enumerations were destroyed by government order during World War I, and the 1901 and 1911 census records have yet to be digitized and placed online. In the absence of Irish census records, Griffith's Valuation of Ireland 1847–1862 can be searched online at the Origins Network (_www.origins.net_). Named for its director, Richard Griffith, Griffith's Valuations was an evaluation of every property in Ireland, conducted between the years 1847 and 1862. It doesn't offer details on family members as census records do, but does provide a listing of the owner and occupier of each piece of property.

Civil Registration Records — Births, Marriages, and Deaths

Online access to vital records in the British Isles is a breath of fresh air after the inconsistent availability of such records in the United States. In addition, all British Isles civil registration records are open to the public, including even the recent records. England and Wales share the same civil registration system, while Scotland, the Republic of Ireland, and Northern Ireland each have separate systems.

Ancestral Trails: The Complete Guide to British Genealogy and Family History, Second Revised Edition, by Mark Herber, is the best in-depth reference book for genealogists with British ancestry. For online research links and information, *The Genealogist's Internet*, Third Edition, by Peter Christian is another outstanding reference.

Civil registration in England and Wales was instituted nationwide on July 1, 1837. Searching these records is much easier than the painstaking state-by-state process most American genealogists are used to, because the General Register Office (GRO) maintains a national index of these births, deaths, and marriages. The alphabetical index, arranged first by year and then by quarter (March, June, September, and December), includes the surname, first name, registration district, and volume and page of the GRO reference. The mother's maiden name was added to the birth index in 1911 and the spouse's name to the marriage index in 1912. Online access to the GRO or BMD (birth, marriage, death) index is available from the following sites:

- **FreeBMD** (*http://freebmd.rootsweb.com*) — This massive volunteer project aims at creating a full transcription of the GRO BMD indexes for England and Wales. As its name implies, the database offers free access. The primary focus of FreeBMD is the period from 1837 to 1903, although some later records are available. Work is ongoing, and the project does not yet include the entire index. A copy of the FreeBMD database is also available for free searching on Ances-try. com, the project's financial supporter. Both sites offer the same data, although FreeBMD offers links to the original index images; response times can sometimes be faster on Ancestry.com.

- **BMD Index** (*www.bmdindex.co.uk*) — This pay-as-you-go subscription site features the complete BMD index in the form of digital images from the original record books. It also offers full name searching and better bang for your buck than other subscriptionbased sites. Searches only point you to the pages in each quarter where your ancestor's name might appear. You'll still have to view the actual pages — at least one for each quarter per year — to locate them in the index.

- **FindMyPast** (*www.findmypast.com*) — Previously mentioned for its census records, FindMyPast offers pay-per-view access to digitized images of all original GRO index pages from 1837 to

2002. It offers a surname-only search to help narrow down the pages you need to view.

When searching for marriages in the BMD Index, there's a technique you can use to identify the spouse in the pre-1912 marriage indexes. In the FreeBMD index, all you have to do is click on the hyperlinked reference link to view the other names appearing on the same page. If you already know the spouse's name, finding his or her name on that page will help you confirm that you have found the correct index reference. If you don't know the spouse's name, you can use this to help narrow down the potential candidates. When viewing actual index images, you'll need to search the pages for both surnames (look for the more uncommon one first) to see if they appear on the same reference page. This, of course, means you'll need to know at least the spouse's last name. Of course, by ordering a copy of the actual marriage certificate, you'll be able to confirm the names of both parties in the marriage.

E-LINK

RootsChat *(www.rootschat.com)* is a free, easy-to-use messaging forum for anyone researching his or her family history or local history. The focus is on Ireland and the British Isles, but there are also discussions for other countries such as Canada and Australia, plus more-general topics such as photo restoration.

Once you've located the reference to your ancestor's birth, death, or marriage from the GRO Index, you can easily order a copy of the original certificate online through the GRO's certificate-ordering service (*www.gro.gov.uk/gro/content/certificates*). Online fees for this service are comparable to what you would pay in person at the Family Records Centre in London or through the local register office, and less expensive than requesting a certificate by phone, mail, or fax. You'll need a valid credit or debit card to use this service.

Civil registration in Scotland began on January 1, 1855, and returns are kept at the New Register House in Edinburgh. The previously discussed Scot-landsPeople Web site (*www.scotlandspeople.gov.uk*) offers an index and online images of the original registers of births more than 100 years old, marriage records more than 75 years old, and records of deaths more than 50 years old. The best part about this service is that you don't have to wait for the certificate to arrive — you can view digitized versions of the actual handwritten register images online. Certificates of more recent births, marriages, and deaths have to be ordered directly from the General Register Office of Scotland (GROS) (*www.gro-scotland.gov.uk*). Disappointingly, this site doesn't yet offer online ordering, but it does include directions for ordering a certificate in person, by mail, or by telephone. For free research in Scotland civil registration records, the International Genealogical Index (IGI) at FamilySearch, previously discussed in Chapter 4, includes entries from the first twenty years of births and marriages recorded under Scotland civil registration (1855 to 1875). If you do find your ancestor in this database, you may want to confirm the entry by ordering a copy of the actual certificate.

Official registration of births, marriages, and deaths in Ireland began in 1864, although state registration of marriages for non — Roman Catholics began earlier, in 1845. The civil registration index is arranged alphabetically by year until 1877, after which each year was divided into quarters as in England and Wales. There is currently no online access to the civil registration indexes or images for Ireland, as there is in Scotland, England, and Wales, although the government is currently digitizing its vital records. You can, however, order searches and certificate copies through the General Register Office in writing, by fax, or in person. Application forms and information on fees are available on the GRO Web site (*www.groireland.ie*).

QUESTIONS?

What is the best Web site for researching Scottish ancestors?

A first stop for anyone researching Scottish ancestry should be Scot-landsPeople (*www.scotlandspeople.gov.uk*), the official family history Web site of the government of Scotland. It offers a wealth of genealogical data on a pay-per-view system, including indexes and civil registers of births, marriages, and deaths from 1855; records of births, christenings, and marriages appearing in parish registers from 1553 to 1854; census records from 1841 to 1901; and wills and testaments from 1513 to 1901.

Emerald Ancestors (*www.emeraldancestors.com*) offers a variety of vital records databases containing extracts and records from civil registrations for Counties Antrim, Armagh, Down, Fermanagh, Londonderry, and Tyrone. Monthly and annual subscription-based access is available.

Births, Marriages, and Deaths in Parish Records

Before the recording of births, marriages, and deaths in the British Isles became a civil issue, such vital events were recorded by individual parishes in the form of baptisms, marriages, banns, and funerals. The earliest date you'll generally find such parish registers in England and Wales is 1538, although many churches did not begin keeping records until 1558 or later. The recording of parish registers in Scotland, Ireland, and the rest of the British Isles began around the same time. After 1598 in England and Wales, a copy of the prior year's register for each parish was also forwarded to the bishop of the diocese. Known as Bishops' Transcripts, these copies provide a second record of the valuable parish registers, and may have survived when the parish register has not.

The FreeREG site (*http://freereg.rootsweb.com*), a companion to the previously discussed FreeCEN and FreeBMD, offers free Internet access to baptism, marriage, and burial records that have been transcribed by volunteers from parish and nonconformist registers of the United Kingdom. Another free alternative for parish records is the International Genealogical Index (IGI) at FamilySearch, which includes information collected and transcribed from parish registers from the British Isles by the Church of Jesus Christ of Latter-day Saints. Both sources offer a good avenue for locating information from parish registers online, but because they are transcriptions you may want to check the information you find against the original parish register (or a microfilm or digital copy of the original) to verify that it has been accurately transcribed.

In addition to the previously mentioned census and civil registration records, ScotlandsPeople also offers access to births, baptisms, banns, and marriages from old parish registers of Scotland from 1553 to 1854. The Emerald Ancestors site, previously discussed for Irish vital records, offers entries from a selection of parish registers for the period 1796 to 1924.

The Rest of Europe

Online genealogy research in Europe has made rapid advancements in recent years, with hundreds of documents and databases being placed on the Internet by local governments and various organizations. Vital records from the Netherlands, passenger records from Germany, and civil and parish registers from France are all available online once you learn where to look.

Ferret Out Family History in France

The French approach family history with a passion, which you'll soon find evident as you start to familiarize yourself with the many available genealogy projects and databases for this country. The records are fairly well preserved, despite several wars and social upheaval, and date back well into the sixteenth century. The biggest drawback to French genealogy on the Internet is that most of the databases, records, and Web sites are only available in French. Don't let this scare you away, however. With a good French genealogy word list and the help of online translation tools you'll soon be able to navigate your way around French records.

E-LINK

Many départemental archives in France have digitized civil, parish, and census records and have made them available online for free viewing. You can find a comprehensive listing of these online resources in the French Genealogy Records Online section at About.com

Genealogy
(http://genealogy.about.com/od/french_records).

You'll also want to familiarize yourself with the geopolitical divisions in France. Instead of counties, you'll find France broken up into *régions* (similar to our States) and *départements* (similar to our counties). Within each département, you'll find cities, towns, and villages, called *les mairies*. Archives are generally found at the département level, while local records are maintained by each parish and mairie. Départements in France are each assigned a number, so you'll need to learn both the name and number of the département to access appropriate records.

A good place to begin your research into French ancestry is GeneaNet (*www.geneanet.org*), a genealogy community for publishing and sharing family trees, connecting with other researchers, and locating records. While the site operates as a worldwide genealogy database, the primary focus is still on French ancestry. Because the site is available in English and several other languages in addition to French, it offers an easy introduction to French genealogy research. Search by surname and village to help locate databases that may contain information on your family, and to connect with other genealogists who are researching your surname.

Another good gateway site to French genealogy is the FranceGenWeb (*www.francegenweb.org*) portal. Much of the site is presented in French, although some portions can also be found in English. Use FranceGenWeb as a gateway to find online databases and records, connect with fellow researchers, and locate the départemental GenWeb sites.

When it comes to records of interest to family historians, France boasts an excellent system of civil registration records dating back to September 1792. Prior to that time, Catholic parish registers (*registres paroissiaux*) record baptisms, marriages, and funerals in much of France. The earliest parish registers date back to 1334, although the majority of surviving records date from the mid-1600s. These civil and parish records are being made available online, primarily on the Web sites of the various départemental archives, at a rapid rate. The French census, conducted once every five years beginning in 1836, is another useful record for researching French ancestors. These census records aren't indexed, which makes it hard to locate your ancestors in larger cities, but with patience they can provide you with a great deal of information about your family. Check the Web site of the départemental archive to see if they offer digitized images of their census records (*recensements de population*).

Seek Your Ancestry in Italy

There is no central repository for most Italian genealogical records, so the first step in researching Italian ancestors is to identify the town (*comune*) or municipality (*municipio*) where they lived. Civil registration was instituted in Italy in 1804, although the Napoleonic-era records are very inconsistent. Once Italy became unified as a country in 1860, civil registration again became a priority of the Italian government. The majority of these records of birth (*atti di nascita*), marriage (*atti di matrimonio*), and death (*atti di morte*) begin in 1866 and continue to the present day. As in France, the predominant religion of Italy is Roman Catholicism, so Catholic parish records provide another excellent resource for vital records — baptisms (*atti di battesimo*), marriages (*atti di matrimonio*), and burials (*atti di sepoltura*). The majority date back to 1563, although some church records begin as early as the 1300s.

There are not a lot of records for Italy available online. You can find transcriptions of selected Italian civil records at Transcribed Vital Records of Italian Towns (*www.sersale.org/comunes.htm*). As with other countries around the world, ItalyGenWeb (*www.italywgw.org*) offers a good resource for Italian genealogy, with online archives and records, how-to guides, and contact information for fellow researchers.

Search for Roots in Scandinavia

The Scandinavian countries of Norway, Sweden, Denmark, Finland, and Iceland offer a wider variety of online genealogical records than most people expect. As with most European countries, the key to Scandinavian genealogy is in knowing the name of your ancestor's hometown or parish. This region's GenWeb sites, accessed through CenEuroGenWeb (*www.rootsweb.com/~ceneurgw*), offer good introductory information on the available records of interest to genealogists, as well as forums for connecting with other researchers.

A good online source for Scandinavian vital records is the free Vital Records Index at FamilySearch. Click on Search from the main page, and then Vital Records in the left-hand navigation bar. This index contains information from birth, christening, and marriage records from selected localities in Denmark, Finland, Norway, and Sweden. The collection includes approximately 3.6 million birth or christening records and 1 million marriage records.

The Norwegian Historical Data Centre at the University of Tromsø (*www.rhd.uit.no/indexeng.html*) is working to computerize many of the historical records of Norway. The site offers free access to the complete Norwegian census of 1865 and 1900, and digitization of the 1875 census is underway. This source also offers access to selected parish registers and other genealogical sources from the eighteenth and nineteenth centuries.

In Sweden, the best site for online genealogy research is Genline (*www.genline.com*), where you can access digitized images of original Swedish parish registers on a subscription basis. The site is available in English, so you can easily identify which parish registers are available before plunking down money for a subscription. You can also buy a twenty-four-hour demo subscription for a reasonable price.

Swedish church records are also available online, again for a fee, from the Swedish National Archives (*www.svar.ra.se*). This site also offers the complete 1900 census of Sweden and a few other smaller databases of interest. A portion of the 1880 census has also been completed. Look for a link at the top of the home page to an English version of the site.

The online database of the DIS Computer Genealogy Society of Sweden (*www.dis.se*) contains over 16.5 million records of Swedes born before 1905 submitted by members. Searches of this database are free, but only members can access the full details. This site also offers an Englishlanguage version.

The *Family Tree Guide Book to Europe* by Erin Nevius and the editors of *Family Tree Magazine* provides beginner-friendly guidance for anyone researching European ancestors, with fourteen chapters each devoted to a specific country or region of Europe. The third edition of Angus Baxter's *In Search of Your European Roots* is another good resource, with ideas for using various research approaches and sources in the countries of Europe.

In Denmark, the Danish Data Archives (*www.dda.dk*) features a number of online databases including a probate index, some census records, and an immigrants database. Look for a small link to these databases on the site home page. The site also includes a link to the Danish Emigration Archives (*www.emiarch.dk*), where you can search a database of emigration lists compiled by the Copenhagen Police from 1869 to 1940 (the database only includes the years up to 1908). These lists give the last name, last residence, age, year of emigration, and first destination of almost 400,000 emigrants from Denmark.

As you might expect in such a remote country, almost every member of the 300,000 population of Iceland is related to one another. You can check this claim out for yourself at Islendingabok (*www.islendingabok.is*). Meaning "Book of Icelanders," the database includes Icelandic family trees and genealogies going back for more than 400 years, covering the roughly 720,000 individuals who were born in Iceland at some point in time. Unfortunately, only Icelanders are allowed access to this database.

Dig Deep for Your German Roots

Many genealogists believe that it can be harder to trace your roots in Germany than in any other European country because of changing boundaries and the destruction of records during the two world wars. Germany as it is known today wasn't even established until 1870, and German descent is no guarantee that your roots reach back to

Germany at all. Instead you may find them in Poland, Ukraine, the Czech Republic, Slovakia, Russia, Hungary, Yugoslavia, or Lithuania. Even small portions of Belgium, Denmark, and France were obtained from German territory in 1919.

ALERT!

Germans to America, edited by Ira Glazier and P. William Filby, is a sixty-seven-volume set of books indexing German arrivals to America between 1850 and 1897. A second series covers the 1840s. This series can be found at many major libraries — a partial list of libraries that have them can be found on Genealogy.net (*www.genealogienetz.de/misc/emig /gta-holdings.html*).

That being said, there are several good sources of German genealogical information available online. Genealogy.net (*www.genealogienetz.de*) sponsors a variety of mailing lists, lists German genealogical societies, and links to a number of helpful databases. Some portions of the site are only available in German. Bremen Passenger Lists (*www.schiffslisten.de*) offers a searchable database of passenger departure records from Bremen for the years 1920 to 1939. All surviving records from this time period — 2,851 out of 4,420 lists — have been transcribed and made available online by the genealogical society Die Maus.

For further research links to German genealogy on the Internet, check out the GermanRoots Web site (*www.germanroots.com*) maintained by genealogist Joe Beine. It includes a comprehensive list of links to online genealogy records, books, and other resources, as well as a basic research guide for German genealogy.

Explore Your Eastern and Central European Heritage

For most of the remaining European countries, access to online records is a bit limited. The Internet still comes in handy for research in the countries of eastern and central Europe, however. Online you can find a wealth of information on the changing political and geographical boundaries of the region, as well as maps, historical documents, and opportunities for connecting with other people researching your surnames.

Begin your search at the site of the Federation of East European Family History Societies (FEEFHS) (*www.feefhs.org*), which is geared toward assisting North Americans in tracing their ancestry back to a European homeland. The site offers links to participating member societies, maps, and helpful online databases for research in Eastern Europe. It also includes a useful collection of ethnic, religious, and national cross-indexes. Another excellent starting point is the EastEuropeGenWeb Project (*www.rootswebcom/~easeurgw*) where you can access queries, family histories, and source records, as well as connect to the country GenWeb sites, from Albania to Yugoslavia. For the countries of central Europe, you'll find many of the same resources at CenEuroGenWeb (*www.rootsweb.com/~ceneurgw*).

If you have the name of the town or village in central or eastern Europe where your ancestors originated, ShtetlSeeker (*www.jewishgen.org/ShtetlSeeker/LocTown.asp*) can help you determine its present-day location.

Moving on to country-specific databases and resources, the Polish Records Transcription Project (*www.rootsweb.com/~polwgw/transcribe.html*) at PolandGenWeb offers access to birth, marriage, and death records for many towns in Poland. The PolandGenWeb archives also include links to transcriptions of a few Polish cemeteries and other helpful information. Additional records for Polish genealogy research, including maps, gazetteers, obituary indexes, and cemetery listings can be accessed at PolishRoots (*www.polishroots.com*). While there, check out the popular SurnameSearch registry, where you can register the surname you are researching and access a variety of surname databases.

For individuals with roots in what was Czechoslovakia prior to 1993 and is now Slovakia or the Czech Republic, It's All Relative (*www.iarelative.com*) includes a great deal of information on surnames, places, and databases to help you search your Czech, Bohemian, Moravian, Slovak, Lemko, or Carpatho-Rusyn family history. Other helpful sites for this area of Eastern Europe include the Carpatho-Rusyn Genealogy Web Site (*www.rusyn.com*), the Carpathian Connection (*www.tccweb.org*), and Cyndi's List (*www.cyndislist.com/czech.htm*), which offers links to hundreds of additional resources for researching ancestors from the Czech Republic and Slovakia.

ALERT!

A number of free genealogy word lists have been compiled and placed online to help researchers tackle reading genealogical documents in French, German, Spanish, and other popular languages. These lists help researchers quickly identify common genealogy-related words, dates, and phrases along with their English translations. You can find a number online at FamilySearch (*www.familysearch.org*) by clicking the Search tab and then clicking the link to Research Helps, or at About.com Genealogy (*http://genealogy.about.com/od/foreign_word_lists*).

A collection of several hundred small databases and records useful for researching ancestry in the Eastern and Central European countries of Austria, Hungary, Poland, Russia, Slovakia, and Ukraine is available for searching at the subscription-based WorldVitalRecords (*www.worldvitalrecords.com*) site.

Swiss family history is best begun at Swiss Genealogy on the Internet (*www.swissgenealogie.ch*) where you can find an introduction to researching Swiss ancestors, the Register of Swiss Surnames, and links to Web sites about Swiss families. Another useful site is Swiss Roots (*www.swissroots.org*), which serves as a gateway for Americans of Swiss descent looking to discover their ancestors. Here you can access a small handful of useful databases, learn a little about Swiss history and culture, and read about some famous Americans of Swiss descent.

Australia and New Zealand

Like the United States, Australia and New Zealand are fairly young countries where the majority of the population is only a few generations removed from its immigrant roots. Government-created records are scattered and inconsistent, and many have limited access because of very restrictive privacy laws.

Records of birth, marriage, and death in Australia and New Zealand are maintained at the state or territory level. A good listing of the

BMD Registrars, along with links to the registrars that offer free or fee-based online access to Australian birth, death, and marriage indexes can be found at Cora Num's excellent Web Sites for Genealogists (*www.coraweb.com.au/bdmaut.htm*). This gateway site also includes well-researched links to archives, cemeteries, census records, convict records, and passenger lists for Australia.

ESSENTIALS

Maori are the indigenous people of New Zealand. It is believed that the Maori originally emigrated from Polynesia in canoes about the ninth century to thirteenth century A.D. There are currently a little over 400,000 Maori living in New Zealand, composing about 13 to 14 percent of the country's total population.

In New Zealand, registration of European births and deaths was first required in 1848 and marriage records from 1854. Registration of Maori births and deaths did not become compulsory until 1913, under a separate system of registration that applied to individuals of half or more Maori blood. These records are not available online, but further information and forms for requesting certificates by mail are available from New Zealand's Department of Internal Affairs (*www.bdm.govt.nz*).

The National Library of Australia in Canberra has a special section devoted to Australian family history (*www.nla.gov.au/oz/genelist.html*), with links to state libraries and genealogical societies as well as several databases for online research. These include immigration, military, and convict records.

Many people with Australian ancestry hope to discover a convict in their family tree. To this end, Convicts to Australia (*www.convictcentral.com*) includes a research guide, timeline, lists of the convict transport ships, convict databases, and stories of convict ancestors.

Asia and Africa

The large and diverse continents of Africa and Asia present a challenge for anyone attempting to research African or Asian family history. Very few records are available online. The Internet can still provide a great research tool for learning about the history of the area where your ancestors once lived and for connecting to other genealogists with research interests in the area.

AfriGeneas (*www.afrigeneas.com*) is the largest jumping-off point for Americans looking to trace their roots back to Africa, with records, forums, and mailing lists devoted to helping you connect your African-American ancestors to their place of origin in Africa. Once you have at least identified your ancestor's country of origin in Africa, the AfricaGenWeb Project (*www.africagenweb.org*) may provide some assistance with directing your research efforts in Africa. If your ancestors were from South Africa, spend some time exploring the National Archives of South Africa (*www.national.archives.gov.za*), where you can search an index to several helpful databases. It is important to note that these are only indexes to available records. The actual documents will need to be requested from the Archives.

The AsiaGenWeb Project (*www.rootsweb.com/~asiagw*) includes links to a variety of country Web sites, covering a broad area from

Turkmenistan in the West to East Timor in the East. Many of these sites are actually in need of hosts, and thus provide little in the way of useful information. The best include ChinaGenWeb (*www.rootsweb.com/~chnwgw*) and JapanGenWeb (*www.rootsweb.com/~jpnwgw*). For people tracing European ancestry in India, the Families in British India Society (*http://www.fibis.org*) provides a number of useful lists and databases. An interesting site for those with Korean ancestry is the Korean History Project (*www.koreanhistoryproject.org*).

CHAPTER 14: Putting It All Together

Now that you have learned the basic research steps, processes, and sources used in tracing your family tree, it is time to put everything you have learned into practice — to evaluate what you have uncovered and assemble it into a well-researched family tree; to publish or otherwise share your family history with others; and to protect your family's heritage from possible loss or disaster.

Evaluate What You've Found

Just as with a puzzle, each piece, or fact, that you uncover about your ancestors needs to be evaluated to determine its appropriate placement in the family tree. What is the record telling you? Is the information complete? How convincing is it? Does it conflict with other information that you've found?

What Does the Document Say?

Reading old records is something you'll have to do often as you trace your family tree back in time. Handwriting styles were definitely different, and the writers weren't always very particular about punctuation and penmanship. Words may have had different meanings, and even dates weren't always as self-explanatory as you might think. An important step in evaluating the infortion you've found is to make sure that you've interpreted it correctly.

ESSENTIALS

In 1582, Pope Gregory XIII ordered that ten days be dropped from the Julian calendar currently in effect, and that the beginning of the year change from March 25 to January 1. This new system became known as the Gregorian calendar, and is still in use today. Because of this calendar change, you may encounter events recorded with a double date, such as 20 March 1718/1719.

Even modern handwriting can be difficult for genealogists to read because of poor penmanship. As you go back in time, the difficulties only increase as you encounter unusual scripts and other handwriting oddities along with archaic spellings and usage. You don't have to be an expert in paleography to accurately read old documents, but some practice and experience is a must. Online tutorials can be extremely helpful in this regard. On About.com Genealogy, the Photo Glossary of Old Handwriting and Script (*http://genealogy.about.com/od/paleography/ig/old_handwriting*) includes alphabets and example text for some of the most common handwriting scripts used prior to the twentieth century. Easy-to-use tips and examples are included in "Deciphering Old Handwriting"(*www.amberskyline.com/treasuremaps/oldhand.html*) by Sabina Murray. For help learning to read documents written in British English between 1500 and 1800, the U.K. National Archives offers an outstanding practical online tutorial in Paleography (*www.nationalarchives.gov.uk/palaeography*).

Dates in genealogy documents can cause confusion as well. A date in a marriage index may be the date that the marriage license was issued or the banns were announced, not the actual date of marriage. Along the same line, people often confuse the dates for births and baptisms, and deaths and burials. Be sure to pair up the date with the correct event.

Once you go back far enough in your family tree, you may encounter different calendar systems, including the Julian calendar, French Republican calendar, various religious calendars, and the unusual Quaker system of dating. You may also find archaic usage relating to dates that you may not recognize. The term *instant*, for example, refers to this month, as in "the 8th instant." The corresponding term *ultimo* refers to the previous month. Examples of other archaic date usage you may encounter include Tuesday *last*, referring to the most recent Tuesday, and Thursday *next*, meaning the next Thursday to occur. Dates were sometimes recorded based on their relationship to another event, as well. A common example of this practice is regnal years, where the year is recorded by the number of years since the accession of the reigning monarch (e.g. *2008 is the fiftyfifth year of Elizabeth II*).

Sometimes genealogy seems to have a language all its own. As you dig into older records you'll come across unfamiliar terms and puzzling abbreviations. It is important that you look up the correct interpretation of such terms as you encounter them so that you don't miss any important clues.

Latin terms are the most commonly encountered in genealogical documents, from the legal language of wills and deeds to the Latin records of the Roman Catholic church. The abbreviation *et ux.*, for example, is one that you'll commonly encounter, from the Latin words *et uxor*, meaning "and spouse." Most of these words can be easily looked up online; check out the extensive Latin genealogical word list at FamilySearch (*www.familysearch.org/eng/Search/RG/guide/WLLatin.asp*) or consult a Latin-English dictionary. Other archaic and obsolete terms, such as those commonly used to describe occupations and medical conditions, can also be looked up online. Try a Google search for the unrecognized term, or browse through the variety of online specialized dictionaries created for this purpose (search for *old occupations* or *archaic medical terms* to find such dictionaries and glossaries).

Prove Your Argument

Proof in genealogy is very rarely an absolute. The facts that you uncover about your family tree may be used as evidence to support your conclusions, but you can really only call it proof if you and others find it convincing. A census record that lists your great-grandma living on her own as a widow certainly provides evidence that her husband is deceased. It isn't proof, however. The census enumerator may have made a mistake in entering the information, or the woman may have stated that she was a widow for any number of personal reasons. The evidence is there, but it isn't convincing enough to be considered proof when considered on its own.

QUESTIONS?

I'm just doing this for my family. Why all the fuss over sources and evidence?

What difference does it make whether Great-grandma died in Georgia or Alabama? Or where the birth date for Grandpa came from? Like anything else, family history is really only worth doing if you're interested in doing it well.

> The best way to honor your ancestors is to represent them correctly and take pride in your work.

So what constitutes proof? Genealogists define proof as a combination of the evidence and reasoning that convincingly supports a conclusion. Evidence alone doesn't constitute proof. A single document can, on occasion, offer enough evidence to present a reasonable conclusion. Yet, the "proof" exists not only in the document itself, but also in the fact that other reasonable sources were searched and no conflicting evidence was found.

You'll often encounter situations in your research where several elements of direct evidence conflict with each other. On the other hand, there will also be circumstances where no individual piece of evidence explicitly provides the information you seek. In these cases, the "proof" comes from analyzing each piece of evidence and creating a logical argument as to why the information, when taken together, carries enough weight to support your conclusion. This is a *proof argument*, a detailed discussion of the problem, the evidence for and against your conclusion, and the resolution of the problem. To assist genealogists in determining whether their evidence and reasoning is sufficient to support their conclusions, the Board for Certification of Genealogists has defined a series of five elements that need to be met before a conclusion can be considered satisfactorily credible or "proven." Known collectively as the "Genealogical Proof Standard," the five steps are:

- Reasonably exhaustive search for a wide range of high-quality sources

- Complete and accurate citation of sources

- Analysis and correlation of the collected information

- Resolution of any conflicting evidence

- Soundly reasoned, coherently written conclusion

A genealogical conclusion that meets this standard of proof can be considered convincing or "proved." This still doesn't imply that your conclusion is true or absolute, just that it is the most logical given the presented evidence.

ALERT!

The Board for Certification of Genealogists (BCG) offers quality examples of genealogies, proof arguments, and research reports prepared by board-certified genealogists on its Sample Work Products page (*www.bcgcertification.org/skillbuilders/worksamples.html*). Other good discussions and examples of proof arguments and proof summaries can be found in *The BCG Genealogical Standards Manual*, and Christine Rose's book *Genealogical Proof Standard, Building a Solid Case*, Second Edition.

You Can't Find Them! Now What?

In the process of researching your family history, you'll likely encounter research problems that just don't seem to have a solution. Perhaps your ancestor has a common name, making it impossible to sort him out from all the other men by that name that appear in the records. Maybe your ancestors pulled a disappearing act between the 1880 and 1900 U.S. census. Or maybe you have followed your ancestors back to the point at which they "crossed the pond," only to have their trail sink into the Atlantic. What's the next step?

- **Retrace your steps.** Review the information you have already collected. You've probably learned many new things since you first started tracing your family tree, and the information may reveal new facts when you look at it with fresh eyes. There may be names that had no significance when you first encountered them, or you may be able to better read the old handwriting now that you've had some practice. New sources also come online every day, so take time to retrace some of your Internet searches and revisit your favorite database sites to see what's new.

- **Check your facts.** Are you looking for the right name? In the right place? For the right person? Many brick walls are built from incorrect assumptions. If you have used a lot of compiled databases or published sources to construct your family tree, go back and check them against original documents. If your ancestors lived near a county line, check the neighboring county for records. Investigate all potential name variations for your ancestor as well — not just various spellings of the surname, but given-name alternatives including initials, middle names, and nicknames.

- **Branch out sideways.** The cluster genealogy technique first introduced back in Chapter 1 really comes in handy when your research hits a dead end. This is especially true in cases where ancestors seem to have disappeared. Because family, neighbors, and friends often moved together, you may find a clue to their former home or their new location by tracing the movements of the people with whom your ancestors had a connection. When you can't find an ancestor in a particular census, for example, conduct a search for their neighbors from the previous or succeeding census. This technique also works well for passenger lists.

- **Don't do all of your research online.** For every genealogical record and source available online, there are hundreds more tucked away in archives, libraries, courthouses, and other offline repositories. The Internet is very valuable as a research tool, especially for the survey phase, but you can't use it as your only resource in a thorough family history search. Use online catalogs and other resources discussed throughout this book to become familiar with other potential sources of information about your family located offline, and then visit or write to the repository, or hire a researcher to do it for you.

ESSENTIALS

If you're serious about genealogy, *Professional Genealogy: A Manual for Researchers, Writers, Editors, Lecturers, and Librarians*, edited by Elizabeth Shown Mills, is a must-have for your genealogy bookshelf. Two dozen leading professional genealogists contributed their expertise to this book. The chapters titled "Research Procedures," "Evidence Analysis," and "Proof Arguments and Case Studies" are especially helpful for their discussion of research methods with real-life examples.

One of the best ways to learn successful genealogical research methods is by reading and studying published case studies. These real-life examples are written by genealogists to describe a particular research process, and the method by which they arrived at their conclusions. Many explore particularly knotty or confusing research situations, so they can be full of creative searching ideas. Numerous genealogical case studies and articles online even specifically offer advice on getting past genealogical brick walls. Michael John Neill has written two articles that may help inspire your creativity, titled "Brick Walls from A to Z" (*www.rootdig.com/adn/brickwall_a_z.html*) and "More Brick Walls, A to Z" (*www.ancestry.com/learn/library/article.aspx?article=11723*). In addition, his article listings at Rootdig.com (*www.rootdig.com/adn/*) include quite a few case studies and other real-life examples of working through apparent research dead ends. At About.com Genealogy you'll find "Brick Wall Strategies for Tracing Dead-End Family Trees" (*http://genealogy.about.com/od/basics/a/brick_walls.htm*), as well as several case studies (*http://genealogy.about.com/od/case_studies/*).

Other excellent examples include "Building a Case When No Record 'Proves' a Point" (*www.ancestry.com/learn/library/article.aspx?article=803*) by Elizabeth Shown Mills, CG, CGL, FASG, and "You Never Know Who You Will Find (While Taking Another Look at the Census)" (*www.ancestry.com/learn/library/article.aspx?article=5542*) by George G. Morgan. These are just two of the hundreds of excellent how-to articles in the free Ancestry Library (*www.ancestry.com/learn/library/archive.aspx*). Juliana Case has also written many thoughtful and entertaining case studies for Ancestry, so search for her articles in the Ancestry Library as well. You should also check out the list of case studies and human interest stories by Megan Smolenyak, linked to or published on her Web site Honoring Our Ancestors (*www.honoringourancestors.com/library_casestudies.html*).

Genealogy magazines and society quarterlies and journals are also filled with case studies demonstrating a variety of research skills and strategies.

Protect Your Family History from Disaster

If you had to evacuate your house and only had minutes to get out, what would you take? The boxes of photos in the back of your bedroom closet? The photo albums on the coffee table in your family room? The computer in your study? The genealogy files in your basement? The old family videos... hmm, where are they? In a disaster situation you often won't have time to grab much, and generally won't have time to go looking. You may not even be home when disaster strikes, which leaves you no time at all. Important pieces of your family history, even those that had survived for centuries, could be gone in an instant. Just ask the victims of Hurricane Katrina.

Back Up Your Computer Files

In the age of the Internet people have come to rely on their computers for everything from online banking to digital photo storage. The downside of this reliance on technology, however, is that catastrophes such as fire, theft, computer viruses, and hardware failure can cause you to lose years of hard work or irreplaceable memories in an instant. Don't make the mistake of believing that it won't happen to you. It happens more often than you might think. But the results don't have to be catastrophic if you back up your genealogy files and digital documents on a regular basis.

There are a wide variety of backup options available, and with technology changing constantly it's probably best to explore these online. CD-ROMs work for small files, and most people already have a CD burner in their computer. For video or large photo collections, you'll want to look at DVD burners, USB flash drives, and external hard drives.

Online backup services offer another easy method for backing up your precious computer files and digital photos. You can store your data offline, away from your home where a disaster might strike both your computer and your backups at once, and use automatic scheduling of backups so there is no more forgetting to back up your files. Cost is a factor in such services, however. ConsumerSearch recommends the best online backup services (*www.consumersearch.com/www/internet/online-backup-services/reviews.html*) based on their appraisal and rating of a number of online reviews.

Duplicate and Distribute

Sharing your family history with relatives is one of the best ways to assure that nothing important is ever lost. Make copies of precious photos and documents and mail them off to family members. Send relatives a GEDCOM of your family tree file. Create a genealogy Web site for disseminating your research. Upload your photos to an online photo-sharing service. All of these steps take a little time, but will ultimately safeguard your family history from potential disaster. Your family members will appreciate the gifts as well!

Don't Overlook the Hidden Dangers

Light, temperature, moisture, pollutants, and the odd bug or two all threaten the survival of family heritage. The solution doesn't have to be complicated, however. Basically, it's a matter of making the time to transfer your photos, documents, wedding dress, family bible, and other family heirlooms into archival-safe boxes, albums, and storage containers. Once they're appropriately packed, they just need a safe home. Find a spot in your house that maintains normal indoor temperature year-round and is generally dark and dust free, such as a closet shelf, a storage trunk, or even under the bed. If you're in a flood-prone area, keep things above known flood levels. You should almost always avoid the attic, basement, and garage because they tend to experience large variations in temperature and moisture.

Information and supplies for proper storage and preservation of family photographs and documents are easy to locate online. Experts at the National Archives answer questions on storing photographic prints, when to remove photos from an old album, and how to safely attach photos or memorabilia to album or scrapbook pages on their Caring for Your Family Archives Web page (*www.archives.gov/preservation/family-archives*). Archivist Sally Jacobs offers ongoing practical tips for genealogists and others interested in preserving their family's heritage on her entertaining blog, the Practical Archivist (*http://practicalarchivist.blogspot.com*).

ALERT!

For small, occasional offline backups of important files, such as your family tree file, sign up for a free e-mail account through a service that offers online e-mail storage and e-mail the file to yourself. At the time of writing, Gmail (offered through Google), Yahoo! Mail, AOL, and Microsoft's Live-Mail all offer anywhere from 2GB to unlimited storage of online e-mail. That's enough space to store plenty of documents and photos.

Publish Your Family History

One of the joys of researching your family history is sharing the results. Family trees can be displayed and presented in a wide variety of ways. A beautiful framed chart can be hung on your wall or presented as a gift. The stories of your ancestors can come to life through a published family history book. Old family photos can take on new life as a scrapbook. Your family history can reach a wide audience through a genealogy Web site or blog.

Write It Down

A written family history can be as short and simple or as long and detailed as you want. To most family members, it will be priceless, regardless of the size or complexity. The first step is to decide what you want your family history to be. Will you begin with an ancestral couple and document all of their descendants, or work your way back up your own direct line? How many generations will your family history cover? Will you include family photographs? Who will buy your book or whom do you plan to share it with?

Once you've decided on some of the basics, the Internet offers a wide range of resources to assist you with your project. GenWriters (*www.genwriters.com/write.html*) has pulled many of these together in one place, with links to a variety of how-to articles and tips, plus a bibliography of family history writing guides.

If you don't want to do the writing or layout yourself, you can hire an individual or company to prepare your family history for you. Search for *family history publishers* or *genealogy book printer* to find companies that can help you with your project. If you're looking for someone to actually write the book for you, the member directory of the Association of Professional Genealogists (*www.apgen.org*)

includes listings for quite a few genealogists who specialize in this area.

Scrapbooking Your Family History

With scissors, glue, pens, and maybe a few die-cuts and stickers, you can quickly spice up your collection of old family photos, and share your family story at the same time. Scrapbooking doesn't have to be fancy. The wide variety of specialty charms, stickers, papers, and other scrapbooking supplies available can certainly jazz things up, but journaling is what makes your history really come alive. Tell the who, when, and what behind every photo and you've done the most important part.

There are hundreds of helpful tutorials, templates, journaling suggestions, and theme ideas for family history scrapbooks to be found online. The Scrapbooking site at About.com (*http://scrapbooking.about.com*) will get you started with the basics, including demonstration of a variety of scrapbooking techniques, and enough layout and design ideas and links to scrapbooking suppliers to keep you busy for years.

If you prefer computers to paper, you can create scrapbooks digitally as well, with special scrapbooking software or a graphics software program. At About.com Graphics Software (*http://graphicssoft.about.com/od/digitalscrapbooking*) you can learn all about this newer form of scrapbooking, including how to choose and use software, enjoy dozens of free downloadable scrapbooking kits, and find links to free online tutorials, downloads, and patterns all over the Web. The Creative Genealogy blog (*http://creativegenealogy.blogspot.com*) by Jasia is an excellent place to find unique and beautiful digital scrapbooking kits with a family history theme.

Share Your Family History Online

Probably the easiest way to share your family history online is to publish your pedigree to one of the popular online pedigree databases such as RootsWeb WorldConnect (*http://worldconnect.rootsweb.com*), Ancestry Family Tree (*http://trees.ancestry.com*), FamilySearch Pedigree Resource File (*www.familysearch.org*), or GenCircles (*www.gencircles.com*). All you have to do to use these free services is to upload a GEDCOM file from your family tree program and they turn the information into a series of online searchable pedigrees. This solution allows your family tree to be found by people searching the Internet, yet requires very little work or technical knowledge.

E-LINK

Heritage fonts can do a lot to jazz up your family history project, whether it's for printing journaling and page titles for your scrapbook or to add emphasis to a published family history. Free Heritage Fonts (*http://genealogy.about.com/od/fonts*) includes themes ranging from medieval and Old English to the groovy '60s and the Wild West.

Another easy option for sharing your family history online is to create a page on a site that offers a set of easy tools for putting your family tree online — à la MySpace for genealogists. The popular social networking site Geni (*www.geni.com*) is one such example. This site took off quickly after its launch early in 2007, attracting more than 5 million users in just five short months who share everything from family trees to a family calendar, messaging, and photo sharing. Geni isn't the only social networking site on the Internet trying to attract family historians, however. Others, such as FamilyLink, MyHeritage, and MyFamily 2.0, let you build an online family tree, collaborate with your family members, connect with other researchers, and share photos and recipes. Many offer secure, password-protected sites if you want to keep your family history in the family. You can find a fairly comprehensive list in the Genealogy 2.0 section of About.com Genealogy (*http://genealogy.about.com/od/social_networking/tp/portals.htm*).

If you want a little more custom control over the layout, content, and design of your site, you may want to create a full-blown genealogy Web site. There are free hosting options, such as the popular FreePages (*http://freepages.rootsweb.com*) at RootsWeb and TribalPages (*www.tribalpages.com*). Alter-natively, you can purchase space and even your own domain name through any hosting service. Many family tree software programs include nice online publishing features to assist in the process of getting your actual pedigree online in a nice browsable format. For step-by-step guidance, check out the NGS guide *Planting Your Family Tree Online: How to Create Your Own Family History Web Site* by Cyndi Howells.

ALERT!

Web 2.0 isn't really a new World Wide Web. Instead, Web 2.0 essentially looks at the Internet as a medium for collaboration, social networking, and user-generated content, and utilizes interactive technologies such as RSS, wikis, and mapping to accomplish this. Many sites that you are likely familiar with are based on the Web 2.0 concept, including sites and services such as Flickr, del.icio.us, YouTube, MySpace, and Wikipedia.

If you've been online at all you've probably heard about blogging. This popular Web format is increasingly being used by genealogists to share their family history online. A blog, short for *Web log*, is basically a type of online journal, with text, photos, and other goodies. You don't need to know any HTML or programming to use blogging software, and you can use it through a free online hosting service such as WordPress (*www.wordpress.com*) or Blogger (*www.blogger.com*). You can also, if you choose, install the software on your own Web site. A blog varies from a traditional genealogy site by having each entry dated, like a journal, and therefore people expect them to be updated frequently. This makes them a perfect medium for sharing every little setback and success of your family history research as it happens! If this sounds appealing to you, you can learn the basics of starting your own family history blog in "Blogging Your Family History Search" (*http://genealogy.about.com/od/publishing/a/blogging.htm*).

Dos and Don'ts of Online Genealogy

The Internet has definitely revolutionized genealogy. Computerized indexes make it possible to find individuals with very little information, on occasion without even a name. Digitized records make it possible to view page after page of records well into the wee hours, long after the library is locked up for the night. The availability of so many records in one place eliminates hours spent traveling to numerous repositories.

All of those benefits come with a price, however. Ease of publishing often results in half-done or shoddy research. The rush to put genealogical records online sometimes results in inaccurate indexes. The sheer wealth of available information makes finding the little bitty fact that you seek a very daunting task. To help you get started feeling comfortable with genealogy online, here are a few basic dos and don'ts.

Do Look for Source Documentation

Just because you find information online doesn't mean that it's true. Before you accept any statement of fact, look for information on the original source of the information. Many online databases will include a Source or More About link. Family trees will, hopefully, include contact information for the submitter. Be sure to document both this original source and the online source where you found the information, so you can accurately assess the quality of the information and so others can follow your research trail.

Don't Expect to Find Everything Online

Many people begin their genealogy search on the Internet expecting to find their entire family tree online, already completed back several centuries. The trouble is, it usually doesn't work that way. You can absolutely do a lot of research online, but don't miss out on the fun and adventure of a visit to the local courthouse or family cemetery.

Do Your Homework Before Forking Over Your Money

Most of the commercial genealogy enterprises online are absolutely legitimate, but every now and then a Web site pops up with questionable business practices. Search the Internet for user comments and reviews of any Web site, software, or other commercial purchase before pulling out the credit card.

Don't Expect to Do It All for Free

You have probably noticed that certain subscription-based genealogy sites such as Ancestry.com keep coming up throughout this book. That's because even with the hefty price tag, these commercial subscription sites offer much more genealogical information online in one place than you'll find anywhere else. If you have a large family tree or plan to do a lot of research, a subscription will eventually pay for itself in time saved. If money is an issue, however, don't forget that many libraries offer free access to Ancestry Plus and HeritageQuest Online. You can also search out the many free databases and resources highlighted throughout this book.

Do Protect the Living When Publishing Online

Your relatives probably won't be thrilled to find their birth dates and other private information online. Even just publishing their names along with the information on their parents can be too much, since many security systems use the mother's maiden name as identification. Use your genealogy software or a utility program to privatize this information before uploading your data online.

Don't Import a GEDCOM into Your Main Family Tree File

It's best to never import GEDCOM files directly. By taking time to enter the data into your genealogy software by hand, you get to learn about the new family connections. If you do choose to import a GEDCOM file, however, make a backup of your main file first and import it into the backup. This way you can revert back to your original file if the import has unanticipated results.

Do Give Back to the Genealogy Community

When you're first starting out, people will likely help you. After you've gained some experience, say thank you by helping someone else. Answer questions on a mailing list or forum. Do a few record lookups. Take time out to transcribe some records.

Don't Assume That Information on the Internet Is in the Public Domain

The majority of the articles, databases, transcriptions, and other genealogy information that you find online are protected by the copyright of the author. If you wish to repost such information in a blog, or on a mailing list or Web site, you need to get the author's permission. Acknowledging the source of the copyrighted material does not substitute for obtaining permission. For mailing lists and blogs, the best course of action is to use a small excerpt (considered "fair use") along with attribution to the author and a link to the original content.

Do Back Up Your Data on a Regular Basis

Since this was just discussed earlier in the chapter, hopefully it's still fresh in your mind. You do NOT want to lose hundreds of hours of genealogy research or irreplaceable family photos because you haven't backed up your digital files. Find a backup plan that works for you and stick to it.

Don't Give Up

While the Internet exponentially increases your opportunities for locating your ancestors, it can also be an extremely frustrating experience to find just the right search combination. Use the search techniques introduced throughout this book and practice, practice, practice. It won't be long before you'll feel like a pro!

Printed in Great Britain
by Amazon